We're Here! We're Queer! Get Used To
Us! Survival Strategies For A Hostile
World.

Published by BookSurge, LLC
North Charleston, South Carolina
Library of Congress Control Number: 2004105616

To order additional copies, please contact us.
BookSurge, LLC
www.booksurge.com
1-866-308-6235
orders@booksurge.com

REGINA
SEWELL

WE'RE HERE!
WE'RE QUEER! GET
USED TO US!
SURVIVAL
STRATEGIES FOR A
HOSTILE WORLD.

Includes Bibliographical References

Booksurge
2004

We're Here! We're Queer! Get Used To Us! Survival Strategies For A Hostile World.

TABLE OF CONTENTS

ACKNOWLEDGEMENTS

There are many people who helped make this book possible. I'd like to thank Gloria McCauley of Buckeye Region Anti-Violence Organization (BRAVO) for her time, wisdom, and support and for making the National Coalition of Anti-Violence Programs reports with me. I'd like to thank Debra Stang for reading over drafts and encouraging me to keep at the writing process. I'd like to thank Kim Sanders for editing and polishing my writing and for providing the emotional support that helped transform this book from a dream into reality. And mostly, I'd like to thank all the people who patiently and generously shared their stories with me.

For everyone out there who felt afraid because of who they were.

PROLOGUE

Reading through the stories in this book may trigger memories of your own experiences of harassment, abuse, and/or violence. You may re-experience some of the shame, humiliation, anger and other feelings that you felt at the time. Remember that you are not responsible for the actions of others. You did not make that person or group of people abuse you, harass you, violate you or attack you. Be gentle with yourself. Perhaps in the spirit of the stories in this book, you can focus on the things that you did to get away.

CHAPTER 1
The Challenge

Men harass bar patron." "Lesbian couple's cars vandalized." "Supervisor harasses employee." "Gay man knocked out, robbed." "Man attacked in parking lot." Headlines such as these, describing harassment, violence, and physical attacks directed at gay, lesbian, bisexual and transgendered (GLBT) people are staple segments of many local gay publications[1]. We rarely see headlines such as: "Man in brown van decked and arrested[2]." Articles in the gay press about "gay bashings" tend to focus on the message that GLBT people, as a group, are vulnerable to attack because of who we are. Until recently, the press has not paid much attention to the targeted victim's efforts to resist the attack. Let's take the following account for example:

> After having been repeatedly subjected to verbal harassment from a group of adolescent girls in their neighborhood, a lesbian couple living in a large midwestern city found a rainbow sheet attached to a threatening note on their front porch. Carrying the sheet and attached note, the women confronted the girls who lived nearest to them. The next morning they reported the incident to the police.

My partner and I were the targets of this harassment. The local paper actually used my story as part of a feature on gay bashing in the community. Though I described our response to the harassment in detail, the headline read something like "Gay Bashing in Clintonville." The article focused on what the perpetrators had done to us and made us seem like passive victims. The article did not mention that the girls stopped their harassment campaign after we and the police confronted them.

In defense of the gay press, it is important to note that by reporting anti-GLBT harassment and violence, the gay press plays a critical role in our efforts to defend ourselves as a community. They have helped transform anti-GLBT violence from an issue seen as an individual problem brought about by something the victim did into a community issue caused by societal homophobia. In doing so, gay press has helped to galvanize the GLBT community into a political force. However, the time has come to focus on our resistance as well as on the harassment and violence that we face.

Because the press (both gay and straight) has traditionally focused so strongly on our defeats, many of us think of ourselves as defeated and hopeless. As a student in a self-defense class put it, "I can't even imagine successfully defending myself. All you read about in the paper are things like 'Lesbian couple murdered and raped.' or 'Gay man beaten with baseball bat in park.'"

Moreover, like the accounts that appear in the newspaper, many GLBT people hide the incidents that happen to them in a dark, musty corner of their mind. Others can readily describe incidents in which they were harassed or attacked or felt threatened, but do not recall what they did to minimize their injury or get away.

Many people don't even realize when they have fought back. One woman that I talked to, for example, told me that she didn't have any self-defense stories. A few minutes later, she told me how she had decked a guy who had been yelling anti-lesbian slurs at her, gotten out of his car and approached her. For some reason, she didn't consider this to be self-defense.

This book is an attempt to challenge such pervasive feelings of hopeless defeat by presenting success stories shared by a number of queer people. First, I'm going to define self-defense and put the violence we face into a theoretical perspective. Next, I'll discuss the two key elements of self-defense, attitude and awareness. The third section of the book will address responding to anti-GLBT harassment and violence. The final section will address violence within our community, same sex intimate abuse and violence.

The story collection process

I gathered the stories that appear in this book through interviews and documentary analysis. I found interview respondents by speaking with GLBT community leaders, posting flyers about my project at GLBT events and gathering places in Ohio, Michigan, Massachusetts, California and Texas, posting requests on gay, lesbian, bisexual and transgendered newsgroups on the internet and through word of mouth. The interviews were confidential. All identifying characteristics, including respondents' names and locations, have been changed in order to protect the privacy of the respondents. Additionally, I gathered documented accounts from newspaper articles, memoirs and autobiographies written by GLBT people, published works and films about anti-GLBT violence, and studies about strategies of GLBT people in the workplace.

Demographically, ten respondents identified themselves as male and fifteen identified themselves as female. Of these, at least two respondents identified as transgendered. I did not get race and ethnicity information from all of my respondents, but of those on whom I have information on, most were white. Two respondents were Asian, one was Hispanic and one was African American.

In the chapters that follow, I do not mention the race of either the defender or of the attacker. I put the task to you as the reader to avoid using racist stereotypes such as those that assume all attackers to be people of color and all successful defenders to be able bodied and white. While to my knowledge we have not yet managed to gather representative statistics on anti-GLBT victimization in terms of offenders' and victim's' race, it is reasonable to assume that these statistics are similar for those of anti-woman violence and hate crimes directed at other groups. We know from this that both attackers and defenders come in all shapes, sizes, ages and levels of ability. If you want to imagine what the person you are reading about is like, imagine someone like yourself who is doing their best to take care of themselves.

CHAPTER 2
Self-Defense: Defining Our Actions as Successful

At its most basic level, self-defense is anything a person does to protect him or herself from physical, spiritual, or emotional harm. If you have done something to maintain your safety, you have defended yourself.

Self-defense is more than just being able to punch and kick. It can also be political, emotional, verbal and spiritual. When we vote against candidates that spew anti-GLBT rhetoric, or refuse to buy products from companies that promote homophobia, we are engaging in self-defense. When we reject religious rhetoric or refuse to accept the negative labels that society tries to place on us, we are engaging in self-defense. When we confront an acquaintance or friend about making anti-gay jokes or change graffiti stating, "God hates fags" to "God loves fags," we are engaging in self-defense. When we avoid getting attacked or physically resist an attack, we are engaging in self-defense. And when we get away from a partner or potential partner that makes us feel unsafe, we are engaging in self-defense.

Every situation is unique and every person has their own personal way of responding to situations. There is no magic recipe that you can follow to perfectly defend yourself every time. The point of this book is to give you options that you can use should a physically or emotionally threatening situation arise.

The only way to get better at defending yourself is by actually doing it. One of the best ways to get practice is by taking a GLBT oriented or GLBT friendly self-defense class. For information on classes, you can call the gay and lesbian community center nearest you, the GLBT student organization at a nearby university or college, or women's rape crisis line. Impact Safety programs, an international self-defense organization, also offers excellent self-defense classes[3]. While Impact Safety Programs is not focused on GLBT issues, it provides a safe space for dealing with those issues.

But I didn't feel successful...

Many GLBT people have a difficult time defining their actions as successful. It's no wonder that many people feel hopeless. Society at large, the mainstream press, and to some degree, the gay press and the GLBT community focus more on the injustices that we face than on our responses to these injustices, at least at an individual level.

The rigid cultural standard for success also plays a role. In American society, nothing is ever good enough; it is almost impossible to feel completely successful. For example, it's not enough to go to the Olympics. In order to feel successful, one must win a gold medal, and even then, if one's scores aren't perfect, it may not be good enough. Most of us apply this yardstick of success to our self-defense efforts. We think that we should come up with the perfect verbal response that stops a harasser in his or her tracks or execute a beautiful snap kick to the knee, palm heel to the nose and punch to the groin that leaves our attacker writhing in pain on the ground, terrified to attack anyone ever again. We tend to see anything less than this as failure.

For example, Jeff, a gay male in his mid-twenties, and a group of his friends defended themselves from a group of male teenagers by running away. The teenagers began their attack by calling them "faggot" and other "garden variety" homophobic slurs, then stepped on their shoes and began punching them. At this point, Jeff and his friends started running, and the teenagers left them alone. Jeff explained:

> It didn't feel very successful...It would have felt successful had I or we stayed and fought and kicked some butt. It didn't feel successful to run away.

In another case, Sonia, a bisexual woman in her late twenties, explained that she didn't feel successful when she confronted a group of girls who had harassed her.

> I wanted to get revenge or get them to change their viewpoint...getting them to be afraid of us instead of the reverse, making them feel the humiliation that I felt, giving it back to them, or scaring the shit out of them...It also would

have been satisfying to see them feel genuinely remorseful and really sorry that they did it.

We also expect to feel like champions after we defend ourselves, but this isn't always the case. For example, while waiting to get her prescription filled, Alia, lesbian graduate student, confronted a man about harassing the women who worked in the pharmacy.

> I told the guy, 'I think your language is inappropriate and harassing.' When the guy argued with me, I told him, 'I have a right to a non-harassing environment.' He came back with, 'I have a right to a non-harassing environment and you're harassing me.' Afterwards, I felt like shit. I had a physiological response...I felt sick, shaky. And I felt really shitty because of the lack of support. It's like my gut was saying, 'I'm a mean bitch.'

Alia's reaction is not uncommon. Most of us are socialized to be nice at any cost. We are taught to put other people's feelings and well being above our own. When we defend ourselves, we violate these rules. Confronting a harasser or punching an attacker in the nose doesn't feel "nice." As a consequence, it's easy for us to feel that we, rather than the attacker or harasser, are bad, especially if we meet resistance or don't feel supported by onlookers.

Second guessing ourselves is another common reaction to defending ourselves. It's easy to replay the incident over and over again in our minds and beat ourselves up for every mistake we can possibly think of. We obsess over what we think that we should have done or wish that we hadn't done.

It is important to redefine the situation for ourselves by focusing on what we did right and noticing the ways in which we stopped the abuse or attacker or minimized the damage that they inflicted. Sometimes the mere fact that we are still alive is a success in and of itself and deserves to be celebrated. It is important to remember that by fighting back, we challenge a harasser's ability to build him or herself up by humiliating someone else. If there are people watching, he or she may actually feel humiliated instead. Finally, by defending ourselves, we send a message that that sort of offensive behavior is not OK.

The exercises at the end of this section are designed to help you redefine your self-defense experiences. Working through these exercises is the first step towards taking your power back.

What about the law?

It is important to point out here that self defense is not fighting. It is not physical or emotional revenge. The point of self-defense is to do what you have to do to protect yourself so that you can get away. Legally and morally, in a physical situation, you should only fight back with similar force, and then, only until you're not afraid anymore. Self-defense laws and the application of those laws vary by state, and you should be aware of the laws that cover your own state. But in general, if someone hits you and you hit him or her back in order to stop him or her from hurting you more, you are probably acting within the law. It is also likely to be legal self-defense if you shoot someone who has pulled a gun on you. However, if you knock someone out and then continue punching them, kicking them, or if you shoot an unarmed assailant, you have probably stepped over the line and are no longer defending yourself. At this point you are actually committing assault.

Likewise, though it's not illegal, humiliating or making an attacker feel afraid is no better than what he or she has done to you. Self-defense is about taking the higher moral path. Often it is enough to call perpetrators on their bad behavior or bring attention to it. The fact that we challenge attackers often comes as a shock to them, since they assume that we will believe their denigrating words, crawl away and hide in fear and shame.

Exercises

In this chapter, I defined self-defense and explored reasons why many people do not define their actions as successful. In the next chapter, I will go into more detail about the sorts of harassment, abuse and violence we face. In the exercises that follow, please focus on situations in which someone has said or done something that has left you feeling singled out or hurt.

In order to defend yourself, you must be able to recognize situations that make you feel uncomfortable. Often people don't act because they refuse to acknowledge that someone's actions have affected them. For example, one man I interviewed mentioned that when he ate out with colleagues, the group often ordered appetizers. Suspiciously though, while the group seemed to dip freely into everyone else's appetizers, no one wanted to share his appetizer. It was only in the process of talking with me that he admitted that this practice bothered him and made him feel excluded because he, being a gay male, was somehow a public health risk.

Exercise 2.1: Think about a moment when someone did or said something to you relating to your sexual orientation or gender identity that left you feeling humiliated or defeated. What specifically happened? How did this incident make you feel? Would you expect a straight person to be targeted in this way? Once you are able to identify homophobic or transphobic situations, you can start thinking about your response to these situations.

Exercise 2.2: Think about your response to the above incident. If you didn't like your response, be gentle with yourself. Let go of the "mistakes" that you think you made. If you didn't respond because you were afraid that saying or doing anything would make the situation worse, honor that fear. It is there to protect you.

Exercise 2.3: Find something that you can pat yourself on the back for in your response to this incident. Maybe you were able to redefine the situation so that it didn't affect you as much. For example, like the man with the appetizers, rather than buying into the message that there is something wrong with you, you recognize that your colleagues are ignorant and afraid. Maybe like Jeff, you ran away from attackers and therefore avoided physical assault. Maybe like Sonia and Alia, you spoke up and confronted harassers. The point here is to focus on what you did right to either stop the abuse or minimize the damage.

CHAPTER 3:
Anti-GLBT Violence: Why It Happens and What It Means

The theoretical approach I take in writing this book is based on the work of Amber Ault and on the curriculum for GLBT self-defense classes that she developed for The Ohio State University[4]. I focus primarily on responding to anti-GLBT harassment, vandalism, and violence and same-sex intimate abuse[5]. All are used to maintain power and control.

Anti-GLBT Violence

In the public sphere, anti-GLBT harassment, vandalism and violence are used as mechanisms of social control—to scare us back into the closet and/or to punish us for defying gender rules and roles. Anti-GLBT harassment, vandalism and violence are driven by homophobia. Homophobia is the belief system that supports the negative myths and stereotypes about GLBT people. This belief system tends to generate, at an individual level, an irrational and persistent fear, dread, and hatred of homosexuals[6]. Homophobia itself is rooted in misogyny, the dislike or hatred of femininity and women[7]. For example, one of the most widely believed stereotypes is that gay men are sissies or otherwise somehow like women. Putting down or stomping out anything associated with femininity is an underlying cause of both gay bashing and sexual assault[8]. This leaves us with the fact that in order to stop the harassment and violence that we face, we must also put an end to our society's hatred of women.

It's helpful to place the violations that GLBT people face from society at large on a continuum[9]. A hostile environment can be placed at one end of the continuum. You may, for example, see graffiti that says,

"I hate fags" spray painted on a bridge that you cross to get to work. This anonymous message creates a hostile environment. You can easily assume that the message isn't targeting you, but still, it may affect you. You may feel threatened. Anyone could have left it there, and who knows what they would do to you if they knew who you are. A hostile environment also may be created less anonymously. For example, a co-worker, neighbor, or family member may tell an anti-gay joke in your presence. The joke may not be directed at you specifically, but you get the point that who you are is not ok.

Verbal assault can be placed next on the continuum. Verbal attacks can range from strangers yelling "faggot" as they drive by in a car to anti-gay comments like, "God hates fags," made by family members at a family reunion. Because verbal assault feels more personal (it is directed at you), it may have a deeper effect.

Vandalism can be placed next to verbal assault. For example, one man in Columbus, Ohio reported that his car had been vandalized in his garage. Both tires had been slashed and "Fag go away" had been painted on the car and walls of the garage[10]. Other people have found anti-gay graffiti painted outside or inside their house, or have found the charred remains of a rainbow flag hanging on the porch.

Hate-motivated physical assault, and sexual assault, can go next on the continuum. The attacker can be a stranger, or they can be known to the victim, perhaps a neighbor or a family member. Because perpetrators are acting out their hatred, the physical damage can be severe or even fatal, such as in the case of Mathew Shepard, who was beaten and left to die on a fence post in Wyoming in 1998.

The threat of harassment, vandalism and violence lead many people to hide their sexual and gender identities. Unfortunately, this does not necessarily make them less vulnerable to attack. Even straight, married people have been assaulted because their attackers thought they were gay. Further, like rapists, gay bashers tend to attack people who they think are vulnerable, and may perceive someone who is trying to "pass" as straight as even more vulnerable than his or her "out" counterpart.

Same Sex Intimate Abuse

Same-sex intimate abuse, like heterosexual intimate abuse, is more personal in that the perpetrator abuses his or her partner in order to get what he or she wants in a romantic relationship. Unfortunately, same sex intimate abuse is even more difficult to identify and stop than heterosexual intimate abuse due to societal homophobia. Queer people have fewer resources available to them because most laws do not explicitly cover same sex intimate abuse, and many social agencies are not equipped to deal with GLBT people.

Furthermore, even in places where the legal system and local social service agencies are responsive, many people do not reach out because they do not recognize that what is happening to them is abuse. Others are afraid to seek help because it involves coming out, which they fear will result in them being evicted, fired, disowned by family, abandoned by friends, or losing custody of their children. Still others fear retaliation or ostracism within the queer community should they choose to expose a community member as an abuser.

Physical violence is only one way that abusers gain power and control. Other aspects of abuse such as emotional putdowns, jealousy, forced isolation of the partner, emotional explosions, and threats of self-harm can be just as abusive and damaging as consistent battering.

One way that abusers attempt to gain power and control over their partners is through the use of emotional putdowns. Abusive partners often criticize the way their partners look, talk, dress, walk, think, cook, and live their lives. For example, an abuser may say things like "What are you, stupid? You're not supposed to chop garlic that way." "You look like a cow going out to graze in that outfit." "Honey, you're lucky I love you because with a body like that, nobody else will."

Like walking through a mist, emotional putdowns have a cumulative effect. Just as travelers find themselves soaking wet after walking through mist for a long enough period of time, people hearing constant putdowns eventually believe them. Putdowns are emotionally abusive; they hurt us at a very deep level and often have long-lasting effects.

Think about your most painful physical injury that is now healed: maybe you broke your arm or smashed your thumb with a hammer. Do the physical sensations of pain come back to you? Now think about a painful emotional incident. Perhaps you have a memory of being laughed at or ostracized because you "had cooties" in elementary school. Or maybe you shared your dream of being a dancer with a sibling who laughed and told you that you look like a clumsy oaf when you dance. Its more likely than not that you can recall almost every nuance of the pain from that incident: the shame, the humiliation, the rejection, the betrayal, and the feelings of unworthiness. It is because emotional putdowns hurt so deeply that they are effective control tactics.

Often mistaken as a sign of love, jealousy is another means by which an abuser whittles away at his or her partner's freedom. Abusers often accuse their partners of dating or flirting with someone else when they've done no such thing. No matter how their partners try to respond to these accusations, abusive partners refuse to believe them and then blame their partners for their anger. Jealous outbreaks function to isolate abused partners from friends and acquaintances because it is often easier to quit talking to people than it is to put up with an abusive outburst.

Abusers often isolate their partners in other ways as well. They may drive their partners' friends and family away by being rude or by simply refusing to socialize with them. This in turn makes abused partners even more vulnerable to physical and emotional abuse by forcing the abused partner to rely almost completely the abuser for social and emotional needs, thus making it increasingly difficult to get out of the relationship.

Emotional explosions can be devastating, leaving partners to feel like they are "walking on eggshells." For example, an abuser may time his or her partner when he or she goes to the store or to run other errands. If the partner isn't where he or she is supposed to be at the end of the allotted time, the abuser will burst into a fit of rage. Similarly, an abuser may explode if the partner does not do things exactly the way the abuser wants them done. For example, an abuser might explode if the carpet is vacuumed the "wrong way," dinner is five minutes late, or the phone rings after 6:00 pm. But the explosions are not really about the carpet, dinner, the phone, or anything that the partner has done, and the abuser will often change the "rules" without notice. As a consequence, living with an abuser is like walking through a field of land mines so that every step has the potential to set off an emotional bomb.

Other abusers manipulate their partners by threatening to injure themselves if their partners do not comply with their wishes. For example, an abuser may overdose on drugs (or refuse to take drugs necessary for life functioning) right before an important event in a partner's life or threaten to kill him or herself if their partner leaves him or her. The abuser is in essence saying, "You are responsible for my life, and if I die it's your fault."

Violence is the most obvious form of intimate abuse. Abusers may slap, punch, kick, burn, pull or shove their partners. Or, they destroy their partner's things, or hurt their partner's pets or children. It is not uncommon for abusers to force or coerce their partners to have sex with them, force their partners to perform unwanted sexual acts or to hurt their partners (without consent) during sex. During an S&M scene, for example, an abusive partner may disrespect the partner's safe word, rules or boundaries.

The physical and emotional impact of intimate abuse is compounded for GLBT people by the fact that many people, including service providers, believe that abuse only happens between men and women. A lesbian in an abusive relationship may have her experiences discounted by phrases such as, "two women can't hurt each other that way." Based on the belief that fighting is what men do, male survivors may face even more resistance. They may buy into the masculine script and assume that violence is normal. Further, when male abuse survivors do seek help, they may be told things like, "If he hits you again, hit him back, harder," "It takes two to tango," or "You let him hurt you? I'd never let anyone hit me.[11]" It is important to recognize that if it looks like abuse and feels like abuse, then it is abuse. If your partner is abusing you, you need to start thinking about how you can leave.

Exercises

The signs of homophobia are everywhere: in news headlines denouncing gay marriage or parenting; spray painted slurs on buildings that we walk past; in jokes bantered about at work or school; and on the faces of people who show disgust at the sight of two men or women holding hands, or of a person who does not comply with society's gender code for dress and behavior. Because of its pervasiveness, it's easy to miss or ignore homophobia and the danger that sometimes stems from it. The signs of abusive behavior within the GLBT community are not always so clear and may be even more difficult to see. In the next chapter I will talk about how to determine which situations are obnoxious and which situations are potentially dangerous. In the exercises that follow, think about the homophobia and abuse you have experienced and how it has affected you.

Exercise 3.1: Think of a time when you have experienced the following types of anti-GLBT violence. Take your time with this exercise and let yourself go back in your mind to how it felt at the time. How did it affect you?

_____ Seen anti-GLBT graffiti
_____ Heard an anti-GLBT comment or joke
_____ Been the target of anti-GLBT harassment
_____ Been the recipient of anti-GLBT comments
_____ Experienced vandalism because you are GLBT
_____ Been physically attacked or raped because you are GLBT

Exercise 3.2: Think of a time when you have experienced any of the following from a partner or potential partner. Again, take your time with this exercise and let yourself re-experience what you felt at the time. How did the incident(s) affect you?

_____ Felt criticized, putdown, ridiculed, or humiliated by your partner
_____ Felt like you couldn't talk to someone or go someplace for fear that your partner would accuse you unjustly of flirting or sleeping around
_____ Felt like your partner controlled your every move
_____ Felt like you had to walk on eggshells in order to navigate around your partner's moods
_____ Felt like you had to either do or not do something to prevent your partner from injuring you or his or herself
_____ Been shoved, slapped, kicked, burned by your partner
_____ Had a child or a pet hurt by a partner

_____ Had a partner disrespect your safe words or boundaries during sex

Note: if you are in a relationship where abuse is happening, you need to get out now before it gets even worse.

CHAPTER 4
Awareness: Turning On Your Personal Security System

Awareness is one of the two most important aspects of self-defense. Attitude is the other. Awareness involves 1) being fully present in your body and noticing, for example if your shoulders are tense or how you are walking. Only by being fully present can you tune into your intuition that serves as your personal security system; 2) noticing what is going on in the world around you; and 3) knowing how others perceive you and how social situations affect this image. While this book focuses on defense against anti-gay violence and intimate abuse, attitude and awareness are general self-defense concepts and are therefore applicable to all sorts of situations that we find ourselves in.

Our culture equates awareness to that stressed out, hyper-vigilant sensation we have when we are watching thriller genre movies. The background music is intense. We know that possible horrific death is just around the corner. Every muscle in our bodies is tense and every hair is standing up. Our vision focuses on what the camera wants us to see. We silently, and sometimes audibly, scream to the intended victim to pay attention and be careful.

In reality, when we tense up, we start losing connection with our awareness. We engage in tunnel vision, by zooming in our focus on stereotypically risky situations (like strangers, dark alleys, or members of particular groups) and ignoring everything else. Or we focus only on what seems safe and ignore anything that might be dangerous, pretending that if we don't see the evil looking guy wearing a hockey mask and wielding a big knife in front of us, then he won't see us. Either way, we are not truly paying attention to the messages our bodies send us or to our environment.

By tensing up, not only are we in effect putting blinders on, but we are also making ourselves more likely targets. Think back to junior high school when you had to do oral reports, speeches or presentations. Do you remember the presentations made by people who were really shy, really terrified to speak in public? When they gave their presentations or speeches, you could both see and feel the tension in their bodies. You could tell that they were terrified. You could see their hands shake and hear the tremble in their voices. Predators, attackers and abusers read the same body language. It's as if they smell fear and go in for the kill, like sharks after blood. The more you tense up, the more your movement looks jerky, forced and awkward, and the more you broadcast your fear and vulnerability to the world.

Further, if someone does attack you, you can fight back more effectively if you are relaxed. Try an experiment: tense up your arm like you are flexing your muscles. Now try to throw a punch. Can you feel how slow that punch is? Throwing a punch with tense muscles is like trying to drive up a steep hill with the emergency brake on. Now, relax your arm and throw another punch. Feel it glide through the air? It's that gliding motion, combined with speed (which will no doubt be a natural reaction of the situation) that makes the strike effective. Now tense up your entire body as much as you can and take a few steps. When your body is this tense, you have to jerk to move. Your tenseness slows you down like you have a 200-pound bag tied to your belt.

In order to be truly aware, you need to be relaxed and alert. Breathing is an important element of awareness because it affects the amount of oxygen available to you, and therefore affects both relaxation and alertness[12]. In order to be relaxed and alert, you need breathe deeply so that your abdomen rises and falls with each breath. When you do not breathe this way, you are more likely to feel anxious, panicked, angry, or out of control because your body does not have enough oxygen[13]. Ironically, most people hold their breath or take shallow breaths when they are nervous, tense or afraid. You can calm yourself down by taking slow, deep breaths.

Another way to relax your body is to consciously relax your muscles. Throughout the day, stop and focus on your body. Ask yourself, "Am I breathing deeply?" If not, take a few slow, deep breaths. Scan your body, starting at your toes, going up your legs and trunk, out to your fingers and up to your head. Ask yourself, "Which muscles are tense?" and then relax them[14].

Listen to Your Gut

You may not recognize it, but you have a very sophisticated personal security alarm system. It's part of you. You take it with you to work, to school, to the grocery store, into the shower, to bed, and everywhere you go. This security system is often called intuition, a gut feeling, or perhaps a sixth sense. When triggered, you may experience it as bells going off in your head, a sinking feeling in your gut, or red flags waving in your consciousness. When these signals go off, your body is screaming, "HEY YOU! SOMETHING'S WRONG!"

For example, Kevin, a gay male student at a small liberal arts college in the Midwest described the following situation:

I was walking down the campus, down this long walkway....It was evening, and there was this guy coming towards me with a cane. We were the only people on the pathway....As I walked towards him, I had an impression that some kind of confrontation was about to occur, but I didn't expect it from this guy because he was part of a hippie kind of group....But we were coming closer and closer together...and we passed pretty much simultaneously right by this light pole....Immediately after I passed the light pole, I heard this whack; he had hit his cane against the light pole....He barely missed me.

Claudia Brenner[15] shares a similar experience about sensing warning signals in Eight Bullets[16]. On May 13, 1988, she and her partner, Rebecca Wight, were hiking on the Appalachian Trail. They encountered a man that they described as creepy at the shelter near their campsite. As they left the campsite, they said goodbye, assuming that that would be the last they saw of him. After hiking for about thirty minutes, they stopped to check the map, and encountered him again.

I heard a sneering voice saying, 'You're lost already.' We turned around, and there he was, about thirty feet away. We were startled....We had only taken a couple of extra minutes to look at the map and he was there, so there was an uncanny feeling. Why was he walking in the same direction as us?

His hands…were draped very casually over a rifle, which was behind his head, across his shoulders….It looked like holding the gun that way was part of how he was used to walking….

We turned around a lot as we walked. We wondered what he was doing with a gun. There was no hunting season at that time. What was he shooting?

Later that day, Claudia and Rebecca set up camp at a new sight. Motivated by deep-seated homophobia[17], Stephen Roy Carr, the man they had encountered earlier, opened fire on them. He hit Claudia in the face, head, arm, and twice in the neck. He hit Rebecca in the head and back. Rebecca's shots were fatal.

With an acquaintance, lover or relative, it's even more difficult to perceive that something's wrong than it is around strangers. Often the clues are not as blatant, but it is just as important to listen to those clues. Joanne, a young lesbian from a rural midwestern area, described the subtlety of the signals of abuse in an intimate relationship. Early in the relationship, her best friend invited Joanne to spend the weekend with her in the city. Joanne felt like she had to ask her partner, Shaunita, for permission to go. She explains,

Every time I went somewhere or wanted to go somewhere, we did it together. If I said, 'I want to go to the store,' Shaunita said, 'OK, well, I'll go with you.' or 'OK, why don't you take one of the kids.' It didn't matter where I went, from the very beginning, either we did it together, or I took a kid or her mother. In the beginning, I didn't even notice. It wasn't like a demand. It just sort of filtered in, and all the sudden, I thought, "I have to ask."

When she told Shaunita about her plans, Shaunita exploded. They argued about the trip. Joanne explains,

That's the first time she slapped me. She was like, "You're not listening to me. I'm telling you, you're not going. If we're going to be together, you're not going to be out running the street,

22

fucking all these people." She was just screaming at me. That's the first time she ever said anything about thinking that I might cheat on her.

By arguing with Shaunita, Joanne was standing up for herself and asserting that Shaunita's reaction was inappropriate. Nonetheless, she didn't visit her friend and rationalized Shaunita's reaction, thinking, "Well, maybe she's right. Maybe you don't do things like that if you're in a relationship."

With people we know, we have to listen to our alarms even more carefully because it's even easier to ignore the alarms we hear, or rationalize them away. We want to believe that we can trust people we know, so we work harder to convince ourselves that nothing is wrong. We want to believe they won't hurt us. We don't want to overreact. Sometimes things work out fine. However, far too often, when we ignore our warning signals, we find ourselves up to our necks in an abusive relationship.

All of us at one time or another have ignored a signal from our intuition telling us that something wasn't right, only to find out later that something was very wrong. Try not to beat yourself up about this. It's a lot easier to look back at the past and see every mistake you have ever made than it is to predict the future outcome of a single action.

You live in a world that continually tells you, "Trust in logic. Intuition is for fools." In a logical world, people would not attempt to hurt other people. When you ignored your intuition, you were following the dictates of our culture. Forgive yourself and work at listening to your intuition; blaming yourself isn't very fun and wastes your time and energy.

Pay Attention to Your Surroundings

"Tuning out" or getting lost in thought is another way that we frequently disable our alarm systems. When I was in graduate school, I had a professor who was so lost in thought about some equation he was working on that he walked into a tree and broke his glasses. We may all laugh about the "absent-minded professor," but most of us have had similar, if less dramatic experiences. How many times have you gotten so lost in thought that you drove past your exit, walked by the building or room you were supposed to enter, or walked right by a friend without even noticing they were there? Most of us, at times, get so deeply tuned into our thoughts that we lose touch with our surroundings. During these times we are not aware of the world that's going on outside our heads.

"Tuning out" or getting lost in your thoughts is tantamount to turning off the volume to your alarm system. Noticing the world immediately around you is an important component of awareness. When you "tune out" the world around you, you miss the details that make you safe. You don't notice people who might harm or protect you. You don't pay attention to dead end streets and other obstacles that might block your escape, or the doorways, alleyways, side streets, phone booths, convenience stores or other places where you could exit or that would provide refuge if someone grabbed you or began to follow you. Similar oblivious states occur when you are so tired that you can barely keep your eyes open, when you're depressed, or when you're under the influence of drugs or alcohol.

Many of us learned to "space out" and to ignore our surroundings as a way to deal with world that was simply too painful or overwhelming, or as a defense against situations we couldn't control. These reactions are especially common among people who were abused as children. This reaction made a lot of sense for us as children. Few of us in bad situations knew we had other options. Disabling our alarm system so that we wouldn't have to hear its constant clanging was a brilliant coping device at a time when we couldn't do anything to protect ourselves from harm. However, there are things we can do to protect ourselves as teenagers and adults. Turning our alarm systems back on and tuning in to our environment allows us to take advantage of those options.

The sooner that you are able to respond to the danger signals that your body sends you, the better your chances are of getting out of a potentially dangerous situation unharmed. Awareness facilitates this process, giving you time to identify your options and act on them.

For example, one late afternoon, Melissa, a bisexual female in her early twenties living in a large midwestern city, was walking back to her car which she had parked on a seedy side street. She noticed two guys standing in the doorway of an apartment complex watching her walk all the way up the street. This made her feel uneasy. Even though she argued with herself about the dangerousness of the situation, she ultimately trusted her gut and had time to consider several options:

[I asked myself,] 'What am I gonna do?' And I started to get angry because I had been on campus longer than I wanted to. I wanted to get home....I didn't want to just walk back and take a bus or call somebody and wait for them to come pick me up....So I put my bookbag on both of my shoulders and I got my hands out of my pockets and I just got ready. I walked past them and sure enough they came up behind me....I didn't want to get into the car and give them my back because I thought, 'They're going to push me into the car, and they're going to get my keys from me, and they're going to rape me or whatever.' So I turned around and faced them. I looked them up and down. I was just ready....They were probably 12 to 16 feet away from me when I turned around and looked them up and down, and they walked a big circle around me. They cut up into the yard and walked around me that way.

By trusting her inner security system instead of logic, Melissa was able to identify the situation ahead of time, consider her options, and take action. Because of this she avoided a potentially dangerous situation. If you don't acknowledge danger until you have walked into a tree or someone has already grabbed you or started swinging a baseball bat at your head, you have milliseconds rather than minutes to decide what to do and act on that decision.

Know Your Vulnerabilities

Another important aspect of awareness involves knowing your vulnerabilities as others, particularly perpetrators, perceive them. The degree to which a person is vulnerable is based on their various group memberships, individual characteristics, and on environmental and situational factors.

Group membership relates to characteristics such as race, religion, ethnicity, gender and sexual orientation. In terms of group membership, people of color, women, people lacking economic clout, and GLBT folks are perceived as more vulnerable because they are perceived to be less able to fight off an attack and/or they are perceived to be less likely to receive assistance from the criminal justice system[18]. GLBT people are particularly subject to attacks based on group membership. Homophobia, an irrational fear and hatred of homosexuals and homosexuality[19] is a driving force behind much of the violence and harassment that we face.

Arthur Dong, a filmmaker, produced a documentary in which he interviewed a number of men convicted of anti-gay murder[20]. These interviews point to four factors that from a perpetrator's perspective make us vulnerable to violence[21]. These factors are religious condemnation of homosexual behavior, tolerance of anti-gay violence by members of the criminal justice system, cultural stereotypes portraying GLBT people as physically weak, and anonymity.

First and foremost, some perpetrators feel that they are doing their religious duty by attacking or killing us. Several of the convicted murderers cited religious condemnation of homosexuality as a rationalization for their crimes. For example, Jay Johnson killed two men and injured one at a park known for cruising in Minneapolis, Minnesota. He explains his crimes:

> I was disgusted with what I was doing [having sex with men]. And quite frankly, I just thought to myself, 'If I shut these places [parks where gay men met each other] down, my temptation to do that would be less.' I would think to myself, 'This is a constructive, moral thing to be doing.' And I certainly didn't just come up with that idea. I watched *The 700 Club* sometimes with Pat Robertson—they're constantly talking about gays[22].

Tolerance of anti-gay violence, especially by members of the criminal justice system, makes us susceptible to violence targeted against us as a group. Several of the men that Dong interviewed assumed that they would get away with their crimes because they didn't believe that they would be arrested for killing a homosexual. Jeffrey Swinford fit into this category. In the interview, he told Dong that he didn't believe that the Little Rock Arkansas Police cared about crimes against homosexuals, and as a consequence targeted them as easy prey to rob. Swinford murdered a man he met at a park where gay men congregated.

Stereotypes portraying GLBT people as physically weak make us vulnerable to opportunists looking for easy victims. For example, Corey Burley, who stalked and murdered a gay man in a park in Dallas, told Dong, "Back then it was the going thing. 'Hey man, let's go over here and rob a homosexual.' You know what I'm saying? We had it embedded in our heads that they were weak. And we could take theirs and get away with it and they won't put up a fight[23]."

Finally, the murderers that Dong interviewed implicated anonymity as a risk factor in anti-GLBT violence. Most of the murderers either sought out and murdered gay men in secluded areas known for "cruising," or allowed themselves to be "picked up" by gay men whom they later killed in a private setting.

The perception that homosexuals are ashamed of their sexual behavior and therefore will not report crimes against them to the police adds another anonymity dimension to risk factors. Donald Aldrich explains:

If you can walk into a 7-11, for 15, 20 bucks, get your face on videotape, have somebody that's gonna call the police; or if you can go to a park, rob somebody that's out in the dark, come away with a hell of a lot more—because of the fact that they're a homosexual and they don't want people to know it, they're not gonna go report it to the police. Who you gonna go rob? Where you're gonna get in the least amount of trouble[24].

In addition to GBLT status, data suggests that membership in any other oppressed group will increase your risk of being attacked. The more statuses you occupy, the greater your risk of being attacked. The few victimization surveys that have examined race have found that GLBT people of color report more violence and harassment than white GLBT people[25].

If you have been attacked because of your GLBT status or any other socially denigrated status, it is important for you to remember that it wasn't your fault. You are not responsible for other people's behavior. Nothing about being GLBT merits violence or abuse. It doesn't matter what you were doing, what you were wearing, or where you were. You did not deserve to be attacked or abused. Taking responsibility for the violence and abuse directed at you and at us as a community takes the responsibility from the perpetrator(s). They made the decision to hurt you on their own free will. You did not hold a gun to their head and say, "beat me up" or "harass me." Even if in looking back, you see that some of the decisions that you made were not the best, that's OK. You can take responsibility for your bad decision-making and do things differently in the future. But just because you made one or more bad decisions does not mean that someone had the right to hurt you.

The point is not to be ashamed of your sexual orientation or gender identity. Nor is it to change your behavior and therefore become less "queer." Who you are and how you are is absolutely fine. The point is to be aware of the risk you face simply because of who you are.

Individual characteristics include factors such as physical appearance, size, choice of clothes, demeanor, physical abilities and body language. Attackers are not looking for a fight; otherwise they would be stalking the biggest, toughest, "baddest" people they could find. They'd all be going after Mike Tyson or Evander Holyfield and leave the rest of us alone. Instead, they are looking for easy targets.

Research on muggers bears this out. For example, one mugger interviewed describes the way he chose his victims: "I was always looking for somebody who looked scared to me when I looked at them. You, know, people give off vibes. You feel this guy looks scared. He'll give it to you in a minute....[26]." Most of the respondents interviewed looked for weak victims who were least likely to resist. However, they did not agree on set age or gender characteristics that marked the most suitable targets. They didn't necessarily choose women over men, or old people over young people[27].

Other research uncovered the specific characteristics that victims hold in common. Researchers showed a film of random pedestrians walking down the street to convicted muggers in Rahway State Prison in New Jersey. Inmates rated the pedestrians on a scale of one to ten on "assaultability." The pedestrians scoring highest on the assaultability scale looked awkward and lacked consistency of movement. The "victims" swung their arms out of rhythm with their legs, so that when they stepped with their right foot, they swung their right arm forward instead of swinging their left arm forward. Instead of the swinging walk that most people have, "victims" plunked down their feet with heavy, clunky steps. Finally, when "victims" walked, the motion of their arms and legs seemed to be separate from the motion of their bodies as a whole so that they looked like puppets being manipulated by inexperienced puppeteers. Other observers of suitable targets point out that "victims" tend to hunch their shoulders and look like they are lost, in a daze, or not paying attention to their surroundings[28].

The clothes that you wear can affect your mobility and thus how you rate as a target. Skin tight skirts or pants and high heeled shoes may look fabulous, but they make walking smoothly difficult. A convicted serial rapist confessed that his modus operandi was to wait under stairs listening for the "clip, clip, clip" of high heels. When he heard what he was listening for, he would attack[29].

Environmental and situational factors affect your vulnerability because they affect the degree of risk that a perpetrator faces in committing criminal acts against you. Of particular importance are the degree to which a particular setting or situation implies your membership to a vulnerable group, the degree to which people can act anonymously, and the overall social tolerance and cultural mindset of an area.

Gay bars, cruising areas and other gay identified areas imply a GLBT identity. We need to be aware of this fact because teenagers and young men looking for queer victims often cruise gay identified areas such as bars or cruising areas to pick up GLBT people to attack[30]. This doesn't mean that you should avoid these places, and it certainly doesn't mean that you are responsible if someone chooses to attack you while you are in a gay identified area. It just means that you need to be aware of the risk that you face in being there.

The same holds true for places like cruising areas and pickup situations that offer anonymity. Several of the men that Dong interviewed either committed their crimes in cruising areas or picked up the victims in a gay identified area and killed them in a more private setting[31]. Just be aware that the situation is risky and listen carefully to your inner alarm system.

Vehemently anti-gay areas and groups also are risky. For example, it's probably not the best idea to go to a militia or Klan meeting wearing a t-shirt saying, "I'm here, I'm queer, and I'm not going shopping." This doesn't mean that you have to avoid all places that are strongly anti-gay. It just means that you should acknowledge the particular type of risk you face by being there.

Exercises

In this chapter, I talked about awareness and some of the particular social interpretations of homosexuality that make us vulnerable. In the next chapter, I will talk about attitude. The exercises that follow are designed to help you become more aware of your surroundings and your own vulnerabilities.

Exercise 4.1:   Wherever you go, play a game with yourself where you try to spot people that you know before they see you. If you see them before they see you, give yourself a point. If they see you first, deduct a point. Score yourself at the end of the week. (This is especially great for avoiding people that you know but don't want to talk to. Since you've seen them first, it gives you the chance to get away.) A variation on this exercise is to use your "gaydar" to help you find people you think are "queer." If you see them before they see you, give yourself a point. Otherwise deduct a point. Try to keep a running tally of your score.

Exercise 4.2:   Every time you enter a room, note where the exits are. Scan the room to see who and what is in there. When walking out and about, note where the telephones are and locate places you where you could take refuge if attacked such as businesses or convenience stores.

Exercise 4.3: Notice people around you. What kind of energy are they giving off? Notice if you feel comfortable around them or threatened by them.

Exercise 4.4:   In order to protect yourself from being attacked, you need to think like a perpetrator. For the next few days or so, when you are walking or driving around, look at people through the eyes of a perpetrator. What are the characteristics of the people who seem like the most "suitable targets?" How do your "potential victims" carry themselves? What are their physical characteristics? Where are your "potential victims" going to be? Where are you most likely to carry out an attack? What about the unlikely targets? What are the characteristics that they hold in common? These characteristics of unlikely targets are the ones that we want to imitate.

Exercise 4.5:   Now, take a look at yourself through perpetrator's eyes. In general, how strong do you look? How do you walk? Is your gait smooth and graceful or is it jerky and awkward? Does your movement originate from a central point or do your legs and arms seem to move separately from your body? Do you stand up "straight" or do you hunch your shoulders? Do you look relaxed and aware or do you look apprehensive? Do you have other characteristics that make you look vulnerable?

This exercise might work best with a supportive friend or in a supportive group. Have each person walk around a bit, as naturally as possible, while others watch. It will take a bit of time to work through the stiffness of being watched, so have the person or people watching time you, and walk for about 3-5 minutes. Also, it is important that the people watching you see you from the front as well as from behind.

As you do this exercise it is important to be gentle with yourself. Notice your vulnerabilities and try not to be hard on yourself about them. It doesn't do much good to protect yourself from perpetrators if you are only going to beat yourself up. Vow to work on the changing those characteristics that you are able to and wish to change, such as mode of walking. In the meantime, tell yourself, "Hmm. This is the way I walk, and that's OK." Most people have some vulnerabilities that they cannot or do not wish to change. For example, you may be vertically challenged or simply love to wear skin-tight skirts and high heels. Just be aware of what your vulnerabilities are, accept them, and be prepared to defend yourself. Tell yourself, "I am fabulous in my 5'1" body and skin tight skirts!"

CHAPTER 5
Attitude

Awareness is one crucial aspect of self-defense. Attitude is equally important. Attitude refers to a person's preparedness and willingness to defend oneself and is reflected in one's body language.

Body Language

Everyone telegraphs information about themselves through their posture and how they hold their bodies. When you walk by or see someone on TV with attitude, you know it; you can feel it. You can see their attitude in their body language. Perpetrators can also see "attitude" and look for people to attack who do not project "attitude" and therefore seem weak and unlikely to resist[32].

You can change the information you telegraph to people by changing your body language. Try this exercise. Stand up tall, lengthening your spine. Free your hands so that they are not shoved in your pockets. Let your arms hang loosely at your sides. Tilt your head so that you are looking straight ahead. Relax, breathe deeply, and take up space. This is a pose of confidence. How do you feel? Now try slumping, wrapping your arms around your body, hanging your head down and looking at the ground. Now how do you feel?

Get back into the confident "pose" again. Just positioning your body in a confident posture gives you confidence and increases your power. You can add to your sense of power by telling yourself something like, "I'm not going to let anyone take advantage of me or hurt me."

Eye contact is another important aspect of body language. Unless you live in New York or some other big city where people simply do not make eye contact with others, it is important to make eye contact with people. Acknowledge others by briefly catching their eyes, nodding slightly and looking away. This is a respectful acknowledgement of the presence of another person and lets them know that you are aware of them. Avoid staring at people or sending them a "don't you even think about fucking with me look" unless you feel threatened. Such a stare may be taken as a challenge and someone may attack you based on that perception. However, such a powerful look is appropriate if you feel challenged. Again, it is important to listen to your gut and follow its advice.

Willingness to Fight Back

Four main factors hinder our willingness to fight back: 1) the cultural denigration of homosexuality; 2) a social imperative to "be nice" and ignore our personal boundaries; 3) the belief that self-defense is wrong; and 4) fear.

Cultural denigration

We live in a culture that denigrates us. The federal government and most state and local governments refuse to grant us the same rights guaranteed to all other citizens. Most religious institutions maintain that our behavior violates religious codes and is therefore sinful. Further, most of us remember the cruel message of childhood taunts directed at those who did not conform to gender role expectations. We heard children, and sometimes even adults, call those non-conformists "sissies," "queers" and "faggots," and got the message that those were the worst things a person could be, even if we didn't know what the words themselves meant. All of these factors have had a profound and damaging effect on our psyches and our souls. We have been told so often and so compellingly that we are sinful, sick degenerates that it is difficult for many of us to believe, on some fundamental level, that we have the right to protest mistreatment.

The truth that got lost in the cultural discussion about us is that each of us is a valuable human being who deserves to be treated with respect and dignity. Any behavior to the contrary is an injustice and a breach of morality. Most, if not all, religious texts compel their adherents to treat their fellow human beings with love and compassion. Further, most of us have received a number of damaging messages that relate to our membership in other minority or oppressed groups and to personal characteristics. It is important to examine and challenge these messages as well.

When people harass and assault us, they are clearly in the wrong, no matter what reason they cling to in order to justify their wrongful behavior. We have the right and the obligation both to ourselves and to society to defend ourselves even if that means hurting the attacker in the process.

Think about it: if a man or woman strikes at you, their intention is to hurt you. There is nothing you can do to force them to throw that punch; they do so of their own free will. The attacker lost any right she or he had to bodily integrity, within reason, when he or she initiated the attack. If, in the process of stopping or avoiding the attack in an effort to get away, you injure them, those are the consequences they have to live with.

Willingness to defend yourself requires a determination to do what it takes to prevent people from walking on, hurting or taking advantage of you. In the worst-case scenario, this means that you must be willing to hurt someone to prevent them from hurting you.

For example, how comfortable are you with the idea of stomping hard enough to break the foot of a person who is calling you a "faggot" and grabbing you from behind? If you find it difficult to imagine hurting someone simply because they might hurt you, imagine that the same person were about to hurt your child or a child that you loved, or even your pet. Would you be willing to hurt that person now? If you feel that you could hurt someone to protect a child or a pet but not yourself, ask yourself why.

Willingness to defend yourself requires that you believe that you are worth defending. Given the cultural programming that most GLBT people received and continue to receive, this may be a challenge. But you *are* worth fighting for. You matter. The world would be a different, less wonderful place without you.

Ignore your boundaries: Be nice!

As children, our parents and teachers instructed most of us to "be nice." They taught us not hurt other people's feelings, not to embarrass others, and not to hit or otherwise harm other children without provocation. Sometimes it meant we had to kiss Uncle Harold even though he smelled like a dead possum. Sometimes it meant that we had to share our toys with a child that we didn't like. We were told that not eating at least a sample of the hideous glob that Mrs. Jones brought to dinner would be rude, even if the thought of it made us want to throw up. In essence, they taught us to ignore our boundaries in order to protect everyone but ourselves.

Personal boundaries are like bubbles that we consciously or unconsciously have around ourselves and are critical aspects of our personal self-defense. Boundary violations set off our personal security alarm systems discussed earlier. If our family or teachers told us to disengage our home alarm systems so as not to bother the police, we would think they were crazy. But when they tell us to disengage our personal security systems for the sake of "being nice," most of us do so without a second thought.

Setting and defending our boundaries is a critical aspect of attitude. In order to protect our selves, we must set our boundaries and actively respond to the alarms that go off when they are violated. Defining and defending your boundaries takes practice. The more you do it, the better you get at it. Reacting to a person who, for example, invades your space on the dance floor, perhaps by verbally confronting them, holding your ground and glaring at them, gently pushing them back when they bump into you, or, if you feel threatened, leaving the dance floor, teaches your subconscious not to ignore other potentially dangerous boundary violations.

Many attacks, abusive relationships and acquaintance rapes begin with minor boundary violations. Gay bashers may begin an attack by invading your space, jostling you around, or making subtle, inappropriate comments to see how you will respond. If they sense that you are an easy mark, they may escalate their attack.

The boundary violations involved in abusive relationships tend to begin subtly with biting emotional putdowns and intensify so that the abuser has almost complete control over their partner. Often, early on in the relationship, an abuser will attack at his or her partner's weak points.

Many acquaintance rapes also escalate from less serious boundary violations. For example, a couple may be kissing and the perpetrator will begin doing something that makes the other partner uncomfortable. The partner will hint or ask the perpetrator to stop and the perpetrator will ignore the request or will temporarily stop the offensive behavior, only to repeat it later on.   In order to protect yourself from being taken advantage of, assaulted, abused and raped, you need to set boundaries and make them clear to others.

The thing about boundaries is that you have to communicate them to people in a way that they can understand, verbally or through sign language or in writing. Say for example, it bothers you that your roommate never does his or her dishes. One option, that seems to be the easiest, is to look at the dishes and utter sounds of disgust or hint that the pile of dishes in the sink is getting pretty high. A second option is to wage a silent dish war by joining your roommate in his or her habit by refusing to do your dishes. Unfortunately, roommates seldom take these sorts of hints. The key is that if you don't tell your roommate that the dirty dishes bother you, your roommate isn't going to know. In order to set your boundary, you need to clearly state it, perhaps saying, "I need you to wash your dishes at least once a day." And if they fail to respect your boundary, you need to find another solution that you can live with such as getting out of the lease or letting go of your dish issue. Similarly, in order for your date or partner to know what your sexual boundaries are, you have to communicate them to him or her.

Stop worrying so much about being nice. Just as turning off a property alarm system makes a property vulnerable to theft, ignoring violations to your boundaries makes you vulnerable to attacks, abuse and rape. Instead of ignoring violations of your boundaries, you need to pay attention to them and respond to them. Just as you develop physical muscles by exercising them regularly, you have to work at setting and defending your boundaries to keep yourself safe.

But self-defense is wrong, isn't it?

Unfortunately, many of us have a difficult time believing that we have the right to fight back. When I was a child, the messages I got from my church and my family left me believing that it was wrong to defend myself. In church, the preacher admonished us to "turn the other cheek" when someone harassed or struck us, which led me to believe that fighting back was sinful. Furthermore, I had an older brother who harassed me when he was bored, and picked fights with me when he was in a foul mood. My parents' response to this behavior was, "Ignore him and he'll go away." They implied that my reactions caused him to escalate his abusive behavior.

Two insights helped me become comfortable with the idea of defending myself, even if it meant hurting someone in the process. First, I realized that the more I ignored my brother, the more abusive he became. My family's strategy simply didn't work. Secondly, I remembered the commandment to "love my neighbor as I love myself." I realized that in order to love my neighbor, I had to love myself just as much; and to really love myself as well as my neighbor; I had to be willing to defend myself.

Fear

Fear is a fourth factor affecting our willingness to fight back. Confronting offensive statements and behavior and physically fighting back are scary. It doesn't matter who the perpetrator is. People in self-defense seminars have been asked what they are afraid of. Most people's responses fall into one of three categories: fear of being rejected; fear of hurting someone; and fear of getting hurt[33].

I think that fear of being rejected is the reason we are so locked into "being nice." We think that people will not like us if we are not "nice." This belief no doubt goes back to childhood experiences in which we were shamed and shunned if we weren't "nice." These lessons are difficult to challenge because we have integrated them into our very beings. It is especially difficult to override these messages and defend our boundaries when the person violating our boundaries is someone we know or want to know.

People who get upset when you defend your boundaries are not the people you need in your life. Those people want you to stay "nice," "passive," and "easy to push around." When you assert yourself, they will try to push you back into that mold. You may lose their friendship when you refuse to be the doormat they want you to be. I know from experience that it hurts to lose those people as friends, but it's worth it in the long run. When you begin being more assertive and confident, you will find new friends who encourage you to try new things and do what makes you happy, rather than discourage you from doing anything but what makes them happy. You deserve to be encouraged and supported.

Another fear that many people have is that they will hurt the person who is attacking them. Here's a reality check. In a self-defense situation, that person you are defending yourself from is attempting to *hurt* you. If you don't stop them, they probably will hurt you. It comes down to you or them and you are far more important than someone who is trying to hurt you.

A third fear that many people have is the fear that they will get hurt worse if they fight back. This is definitely the message that school bullies gave us. They had a vested interest in convincing us that they would really hurt us if we challenged them. As long as we passively complied with their wishes, they got whatever they wanted and didn't risk losing face.

This is also a message that most women have heard for years in regard to rape. This belief is not supported by research. Researchers found that women who defended themselves were less likely to get raped[34]. Furthermore, the men that Arthur Dong interviewed in *License to Kill* interviewed made it clear that they would have killed or at least tried to kill their victims no matter what their victims did[35]. This means that you probably will increase your odds of survival by fighting back. But above all else, listen to and trust your gut. If your gut or intuition says, "FIGHT!" then do so. If it says, "maybe it would be better to lie low for a bit," then do that.

It is also likely that some of the fear of getting hurt relates to a lack of knowledge about how to effectively fight back. Practicing the techniques in this book, preferably with a friend or partner, should help ease these fears. Better yet, take a GLBT self-defense class or a feminist-oriented women's self-defense class. Call your local anti-violence project for information about GLBT self-defense classes (see listings in Appendix A).

Self-Defense and the Law[36]

You have the legal right to make yourself safe. If someone approaches you in a way that makes you feel uncomfortable, you do not have to interact with that person in any way. If someone attacks you physically, you are legally empowered to use physical force to defend yourself. Furthermore, if, as a reasonable person, you feel that someone is about to physically attack you, you have the right to use reasonable force to prevent injury to yourself.

However, the law does not permit retribution or revenge. Self-defense simply means getting away from an attack and incurring as little damage to your self as possible in the process. Once you are no longer afraid, if you continue to beat or kick an attacker, or you come back half an hour later to hurt the person that attacked you, you have just committed assault yourself and are morally and legally in the wrong.

Exercises

In this chapter I talked about attitude and body language. In the next chapter I will talk about how to put these ideas into action by responding to harassment. The exercises that follow are designed to help you tap into your attitude.

Exercise 5.1: Affirmations are one way to work on your willingness to fight back. These are excellent starter affirmations. Tell yourself, "I am worth fighting for. I am worth defending. I have a right not to be abused. I matter. I have the right to defend myself." You can say these affirmations out loud or silently in your head, or write them. It's a good idea to do all three. You can expand on these affirmations, adding whatever you need to hear or what makes you feel good. It might be something like one of the following: "I am completely good. I am completely lovable. I deserve to take up space. I deserve to be loved. I am fabulous." If you don't believe the affirmations, that's ok. A friend of mine points out, "Affirmations are the lies we tell ourselves until they are true."

If you find one or more of your affirmations difficult to believe, go further with that feeling of doubt. Write the affirmation. If you hear yourself arguing with, cynically laughing about, or disregarding the affirmation, write your thought or argument beneath your affirmation. Write your affirmation again. If an argument or cynicism comes up, write that down. Continue this process until your cynical voice gives up[37].

For example, often when I work with affirmations, I write something like, "I am completely good," and I hear myself say, "Humph," or "Yeah, right," or "Bullshit." So I write the argument, which usually is something like this: "If you were really good, X bad thing wouldn't have happened." (I may expand on this argument for pages.) I write my affirmation again, and my argument, which now may be, "You didn't clean the litter box. You are very bad." I continue this process until my cynical voice gets tired of arguing and finally just says something like, "OK, already, I accept it."

Exercise 5.2: Oftentimes, we figure out our boundaries have been violated. The things that make us crazy usually indicate behaviors that violate some boundary of ours. Set aside half an hour and make a list of all the things that your colleagues, friends, lovers and relatives do that drive you crazy. Be sure to write the person's or persons' name(s) next to the issue. Now, go back through the list and specify the boundary that was violated by each particular behavior.

Exercise 5.3: Practice setting small boundaries. Each day, pick one boundary that you want to work on and set that boundary at least once. For example, I hate talking to telemarketers. To work on this, I might chose to screen all my calls and only answer the phone if it is someone that I want to talk to. Similarly, I hate having people touch my neck. So I might tell the people who tend to feel compelled to adjust my collar or tuck in my tag that it really bothers me when they do that and ask them to stop. If this is new for you, pick boundaries that are somewhat insignificant. And remember, the idea is not to pick a fight, so be respectful when you set your boundaries.

CHAPTER 6
So What Am I Supposed To Do About It??? Responding To Harassment

In the last two chapters I talked about general aspects of self-defense. In this chapter and the chapters that follow, I will be talking about specific self-defense issues and strategies. This chapter deals with harassment. Below are a number of harassment scenarios. As you read through them, think about how you have responded to similar situations. How did your response(s) leave you feeling? How do you think that you might respond now?

As you walk out the door of your favorite coffee shop, three guys in a red pickup truck yell, "Fudgepacker!" at you as they drive by.

As you unlock the doors to your car, an eleven year-old boy walks up to you and asks tauntingly, "Are you gay?" The group of boys with him laughs in response.

Walking hand in hand with your partner on an ice-covered sidewalk, a group of fraternity boys behind you snicker and make rude comments about what the two of you do in bed.

A co-worker tells an anti-gay joke and the rest of the group laughs.

A co-worker who is sympathetic to GLBT issues finds excuses to touch you, such as by adjusting your collar and "fixing" your hair. The touching feels invasive.

After discovering that you are a lesbian, your brother-in-law repeatedly asks you to have sex with him, promising that he can "cure" you.

Your 12-year-old sister goes on a ten-minute diatribe, complaining about everything from your parents' rules, the new car your parents bought, the middle school she goes to, and the mall where you offer to drop her off. Everything she complains about is either "gay" or "so gay."

After your grandmother's funeral, your aunt exclaims, "I can't believe he had the nerve to show up. Everyone knows he's... well, you know...." She is referring to a man known by the community to be gay.

Because the remarks and actions described above bring unwanted attention to the recipient's sex, gender, or sexual orientation[38], they are all forms of sexual harassment. GLBT people with additional stigmas such as race, ethnicity, religion, or disability often face harassment based on these issues as well.

When you were reading through these examples, did you find yourself focusing more on how you would like to respond to the situation than on how you know that you probably would respond? If you did, count yourself among the masses. Because we have been socialized to be polite, or at least to not make a scene, most people tend to respond to issues of harassment by one or more of the following: looking away; feeling embarrassed; laughing; ignoring the incident and pretending that it didn't happen; and/or feeling powerless and frustrated. The problem is that these responses often are passive. Not only do passive responses make us feel bad, they send a message to potential attackers that we are vulnerable and submissive.

A healthy response to harassment must occur on two levels. The first level is the internal response. The second is the external reaction. Internal response refers to how we let the harassment affect us. External response refers to what we do about the harassment.

Taking the sting out of harassment

At one level, self-defense refers to defining yourself in a positive manner and repelling the attempts of others to define you negatively. Just as the hideous shirt that someone gave you for your birthday cannot make you a social outcast if you don't wear it, abusive words cannot hurt you if you do not accept them. The key is to define yourself in a positive manner and not let someone else define you differently.

This simple idea can be very difficult to achieve. As children, most if not all of us got messages from our families, schools, the media, and possibly our churches telling us that we were somehow bad because we didn't measure up intellectually, physically, behaviorally or spiritually. For many of us, these negative messages helped to form the tapestry of our identities. The messages littering the social landscape that condemn our gender identity and/or sexual orientation often get woven in with the rest of the messages that we hear, shaping the way that we feel about ourselves. It is because of these negative messages that looks of disgust and words slung as epithets such as "faggot," "bull dagger," and "she'im" hurt. They leave us feeling like there is something wrong with us and make it easy to point to our gender preference or sexual orientation as the overriding flaw. In short, the words hurt because at some level we believe them.

Stop believing those negative messages! Search through your tapestry for your gifts, virtues, and other positive aspects of your character and focus on these. Forgive yourself for what you have always thought of as your "flaws." The body isn't good or bad; it simply is. This is a biological fact. The same standard can be applied to gender identity and sexual orientation. They are neither good nor bad. They just are. It is society that applies the rules and labels. At the most basic, internal level, in order to defend yourself from the sting of harassment, you must pull those labels out of your tapestry. You are; therefore you are worthy of love and respect.

In *Straight Jobs, Gay Lives*, Roberta Lasley explains how she learned to evade the sting of harassment:

> I was marked as an illegitimate kin in a town where everybody knew it, and it was something to be ashamed of. So figuring out I was a dyke when I was a teenager was nothing.... I learned about being excluded in ways that are unfair - because you are illegitimate, because you are fat, because you are a lesbian, because you're whatever the hell it is. Those are the kinds of things that really forge your own personality. The only place you can go is inside, to hear your own voice, because those outside voices are not your voices—they're not real.[39]

Gerald, a gay man who found my posting on the internet explained his process this way:

> I studied Zen for a time.... I shrug when I encounter a derisive or negative attitude toward me. My belief is that it is THEIR problem. (THAT I learned from a Black friend, years ago.)... Don't allow anything they say to "get to you".... YOU know none of it is true. Let it slide off your back as if it simply doesn't exist.

Sometimes the process of disentangling the hatred from one's personal tapestry (filtering out all of the negative messages) can be dramatic. For example, when Donna and René got together, Donna was 17 and had just had a baby, and René was still in high school. They both were married at the time. They were disowned by their families and lost all but one of their friends. The final blow came about six months after Donna and René moved in together when Donna's husband got custody of their daughter. Donna notes, "At the time, we had no gay friends. My parents wrote me off when I lost custody. We literally had nobody but each other."

I asked them how they got through that time. Donna explained the process:

Through the first part of it, we did a lot of drugs. That was the only thing that brought any temporary relief. Finally, several months after [my daughter] was taken from our house, René and I decided on a joint suicide pact. We had a gun and we started fighting over who was going to kill herself first. We were pulling the gun back and forth…and the gun goes off. And I remember closing my eyes [and thinking,] "Oh my God, I've blown my leg off." I didn't feel anything so then it was obvious that she was shot. So I opened my eyes…and she was fine; but the showerhead was dead. We [had blown] the showerhead clear off the wall. And at that point, it was like, "What the hell are we doing? Am I going to let this jerk destroy the only happiness that I've had, which is exactly what he set out to do?…" And at that point, [I decided] no more drugs. Yeah, I don't have my daughter every day, but I've got her 4 1/2 days a month, and that's something. That's what I have to focus on.

René explained how killing the showerhead affected her.

We were supposed to be dead. If we're evil and sinners, we shouldn't be alive. In our minds, it was like, "Ok, we've got an answer here. We are not supposed to be dead."

Eventually, Donna and René won custody of Donna's daughter by watching Donna's ex-husband, recording everything that he did, and fighting the battle in court.

Sometimes, a less drastic ritual can be helpful in unraveling the negative messages from your tapestry. For example, Anita, a lesbian from the Southwest in her early thirties, describes how she was able to let go of the negative messages that she got from her family.

In my mid-twenties, I watched this video of these Native Americans that had gotten together years after their experiences in boarding schools…. They wrote down stuff that they wanted to get out and then they burned the paper. And I wrote [my story] down and ended up with a stack about [five inches thick] of pieces of sayings.

I realized that I was telling myself things, negative things, but it wasn't in my own voice. So I said, "Who was saying that to me?" And I remembered who it was. It was from a long time ago. Things like "No wonder nobody likes you," from my sister as a child. "Oh, but Anita, you always remember things wrong" was from my mother. There were all of these little sayings.

So I thought, "Okay. Once and for all, I'm going to see how many of these things I can come up with." And I'm still coming up with them, but not as frequently.

I put them on these cards and I put a rubber band around them, and I put them in this box [and] put the lid on.... One thing I'm afraid of is forgetting stuff. I figure if I write these down, it's in storage. Anyway, I organized them by who said it and how old I was. And when I went back and looked at them, I thought, "This is awful."

Stopping Harassers in Their Tracks

At another level, self-defense refers to making a conscious choice about how to respond to hurtful words and actions directed at you and supporting that choice through your actions. This is no small matter. Harassers use words, symbols and gestures to intimidate and humiliate us into relinquishing our power to them. They symbolically (and sometimes physically) beat us down in order to build themselves up.

It is important to remember that sexual harassment not only generates power for the harasser, but it stems from a position of power. The fear that we feel when someone yells, "Hey faggot, suck this!" is real, because the risk that we face because of who we are is real.

Given this risk, passive responses to harassment make sense...or do they? By its very nature, anti-GLBT harassment is inherently political[40]. Anti-GLBT harassment is not simply directed at a unique individual; it targets gays, lesbians, bi-sexuals, and transgendered people as a group. As such, anti-GLBT harassment denies all of us our basic human rights. We are not free to walk in public spaces or attend classes and workshops without fear of being denigrated or put on the spot; work without fear of being fired; rent a place to live without risk of being evicted; have children or joint property with a partner without fear of losing them; or attend religious services in the congregation of choice without fear of being condemned. Our rights and our freedoms are denied us one person at a time. In order to win these rights, we have to challenge anti-GLBT harassment one harasser at a time.

On the personal level, confronting harassers shifts the balance of power, because rather than giving up our power, we are exercising it. Rather than feeling vulnerable, powerless and angry, confronting harassment can make us feel powerful while making the harasser feel vulnerable and small.

On the political level, confronting anti-GLBT harassment challenges the status quo. People who harass us expect us to meekly accept the humiliation that they dish out. They don't expect us to resist. Confronting their bad behavior challenges that assumption and increases the risks of harassment. This makes it difficult for harassers to continue their behavior, because rather than getting a reward in the form of a boost in their sense of power and dominance, they pay a cost in terms of being humiliated themselves. Because most confrontations occur in front of other people, confrontation affects not only the individual harasser but also other harassers or would-be harassers who are watching. It empowers other GLBT people to stand up for their rights as well.

The art of confrontation: the basics

The easiest way to do confrontation is by using the following three-step model advocated by the Ohio State University Rape Education and Prevention Program:

1.   Define the situation.

   2. Interpret the situation.

   3. Tell the offender what to do[41].

Defining the situation is simply naming the behavior. It is a little like explicitly stating the obvious. The key is that it involves defining the situation for yourself based on how it feels to you rather than letting someone else define the situation for you. It is important to be specific at this point so that there is no room for discussion. For example, if you're walking down the sidewalk and a bully steps in front of you, blocking your path, you might define the situation by stating, "You're blocking my path."

Interpreting the situation refers to giving a social or political meaning to the objective facts of the situation. What do you think the bully "means" by blocking your path? A reasonable interpretation of the situation might be, "You're blocking my path to intimidate me."

The third step, telling the offender what to do, involves demanding that the offensive behavior stop. To continue with the above example, telling the offender what to do might sound like, "You're blocking my path to intimidate me. Move out of the way."

At first, you may find it difficult to make clear, direct statements without adding fluff, saying please, or making your directive into a question rather than a command. For example, it may be tempting to say something like, "I know you probably don't mean to block the sidewalk, but could you please move out of the way?" You need to practice so that you can simply make a direct statement, without apology, much like you would command a dog that's about to knock over your trash, or a child who's about to touch an active burner on the stove. It is also important to reinforce your response with strong body language. Hold your head up, lengthen your spine, and take a strong, serious stance. Don't smile.

It also may be tempting to take an extra shot at the harasser, calling him or her an asshole, or telling the harasser to "fuck off." You need to avoid this kind of name-calling as much as possible, because it is likely to escalate a situation rather than de-escalate it. Threats, insults and obscenities target the person rather than the behavior and bring the offender's ego into the mix, making it more likely that he or she will strike back physically.

It is possible that the offender will try to argue with you, to challenge your definition of the situation, or try to taunt you for standing up for yourself. When this happens, it is important to keep focused on your agenda. It is pretty obvious that questions like "Are you on the rag?" or "Did you get your apron ruffle stuck in your butt or what?" don't merit a response. Don't give them one. The "broken record" approach is a wonderful way to keep focused on your agenda. No matter what the offender says to you, repeat your original definition, interpretation and command, over and over if you have to. If you refuse to argue, the offender most likely will give up out of boredom if nothing else.

It's important to insert a warning at this point. Members of your family, no matter how much they deserve to be confronted, may not the best people to hear your first confrontation[42]. If your family has always insisted that you be nice, passive, and easy to push around, they may not be supportive of your new assertiveness skills and may try to push you back into your old role. If this is the case with your family, it may be useful to build up your confrontation skills a bit before you confront someone in your family. This way, you will be more immune to their efforts to push you back down.

Verbal Confrontation

The following excerpt from *Straight Jobs, Gay Lives* provides a good example of verbal confrontation. During his second year at Harvard Business School, Douglas Plummer confronted his class about a presentation featuring anti-gay stereotypes made by several classmates and about the response of the rest of his classmates to the denigrating stereotypes. Douglas explains,

> [T]hey did this spoof of this really effeminate gay man who wanted to open up an antique and flower shop, and everyone was laughing....I was just pissed beyond belief. So I raised my hand and waited for the professor to call on me. He asked, 'What do you think about gold prices in Latin America in the 1983 era?' I said, 'I don't have anything to say about that. I want to talk about the video. The stereotypes it portrayed of

gay people was offensive to me, and to gay people in general, and I'm really upset by the fact that everyone in the section laughed at it, and no one made any comments about it.'

The professor tried to pretend as though nothing had happened, but Douglas persisted. He said,

'Wait a second. I have a legitimate issue here.... I want some response.' At that point the section leader stood up and said, 'Look, this is something we need to talk about after class. If it's all right with you, Douglas, we'll talk about this at the end of class.'

Douglas noted that while some people challenged him for bringing the issue up at all, the people who made the presentation apologized to him[43].

Natalie, a lesbian in her thirties living in a large midwestern city, describes confronting employees in a grocery store and then taking her issue to the management. She was shopping at the grocery store in her neighborhood where there was a large lesbian presence.

It was in June, and it was a couple of days before a very large gay pride march in which I would be taking part. I was doing my shopping, and...there were two workers in the produce section who were unloading and stocking the shelves.

One of the workers said to the other worker, within earshot of me, 'Hey, did you hear what's happening downtown on Saturday?'

The other said, 'No.'

'Well it's a big queer march. I think we ought to go get a gun and shoot 'em.'

Being aware of these issues, I thought to myself, 'I can't let this go on and just kinda hang there without somebody challenging it.' And so I summoned up my courage and said, 'That's really not appropriate.'

The person who made the comment said, 'What are you talking about?'

And I said, 'I know you are probably saying it in a joking manner, but some people really do think it's okay to shoot gay people, and that's not all right.'

This guy just looked at me and said, 'I don't think there's anything wrong with what we're saying.'

So I went to the manager and I said, 'I want to tell you about something I overheard in your store.' I repeated the conversation I had heard to him. He said, 'Well, this store is apolitical. We can't dictate the politics of our staff members.'

I said, 'This is not about dictating their politics. It's about the fact that your customers may come to feel unsafe. I certainly feel unsafe as a lesbian who shops here, knowing that these are the kinds of sentiments that your employees are expressing.' About this point, another friend of mine who is a lesbian walked through the door. She joined me...and I briefly clued her into the events. So then both of us were saying to the manager, 'Listen, there really is a strong lesbian presence in this neighborhood, and we're not going to say goodbye to you here until you make a commitment to at least raise this as an issue with these staff members.'

Finally, the manager agreed that he would at least discuss this with the staff. [However,] he remained committed to his idea that this was about politics and his staff was free to express their political opinions.

Body Language

Sometimes body language alone is enough to convey your message. For example, Brenda, a lesbian social worker at a large, inner city hospital, describes how she used her eyes to stop the obnoxious behavior of a police officer who was taking a report in the emergency room of same-sex domestic violence. A deaf, pre-operative transsexual man who had been battered came into the emergency room, dressed in women's clothes and wearing make-up.

He was being interviewed by two policemen, one of whom did know sign language. That police officer was very polite and respectful, but the other police officer kept rolling his eyes and laughing and making snide remarks under his breath. I caught his eye, glared at him, and shook my head. He subsided.

But while I was talking with the patient (with the assistance of the decent police officer), the other police officer started to snicker and make comments again. Meanwhile, the doctor came in and started sewing up the wound on the patient's hand. The ignorant police officer started to joke loudly about how he was glad that patient wasn't pressing charges, because he didn't want to hear any more about his sex life.... I caught the cop's eye again and gave him an absolutely evil look. He said he'd wait outside and left.

Later, Brenda verbally confronted the physician in charge for allowing the officer to be so disrespectful.

After his injuries had been treated and the patient had been discharged, I found the doctor, took a deep breath and said, "Tim, we need to talk. I really didn't like what happened in there." He gave me a puzzled look.

I took another deep breath. "It really bothered me that one of the police officers was treating the patient with so much disrespect. I don't know if it's your responsibility as the resident in charge of the case to say something, or mine as the social worker, but I don't want to see that happen again."

The doctor shrugged. "You mean what he was saying? What difference does it make? The guy was deaf. He couldn't hear any of it."

I said, "Maybe he couldn't hear the words, but he could see the laughter and the disgust, and he seemed to read lips well enough to get the gist of what was being said. That's terrible enough. But even to add to it, you can't always tell who's gay and who isn't. What if a gay staff person had been listening? What if some of our other patients in that treatment area are gay or have gay family members? Don't you think they would have found what happened offensive, too?"

"Well," he said, "those people offend me, so I don't much care if I offend them."

I was shaking by that time, but I pushed on. "As a professional, you have an obligation to see that all of your patients are treated with respect while they're in this hospital," I said, "Whatever you choose to believe in your personal life."

"I'll tell you who isn't treated with respect around here," he said. "It's white straight men."

"I'm sorry to hear that," I said. "If you ever hear the police talking that way about a white straight man, feel free to put a stop to that, too."

Going through official channels

Another way to deal with harassment is to go through official channels and have authorities respond to the incident. For example, Andrea, a lesbian in her mid-twenties, works in a big corporation that at least gives lip service to diversity - including sexual orientation. The overall environment is at least gay-tolerant and many people are gay-friendly.

She explains:

There's this guy at work that I used to not get along with very well.... Shortly after the famous fashion designer was shot in front of his Miami home and people were talking about that, Adam made this comment about how supposedly gay men are really into hamsters, and he was laughing.... I was really offended.

I didn't confront him directly because Adam's not gonna change. And I didn't want to have to be the one who looked bad.... And yet I didn't want nothing to be done about it. My supervisor supported me about going to human resources. The person I talked to at human resources was really cool. She was really supportive and made it really clear to me that it was absolutely appropriate to report that.

It was done really discreetly. People didn't act like I had done anything. They might have figured it out…. but the cool thing was Adam didn't treat me any differently. In fact, I made an effort on my part to be really diplomatic with Adam, not to treat him like I was bitter…just to be friendly with him. And he, suprisingly, was doing the same thing with me. It was like he wanted to make it clear that he didn't mean any hard feelings. And we actually get along really well now. He even sat behind me for awhile and we developed sort of a friendly rapport where we were joking with each other and whatever…. And he hasn't made any more homophobic comments.

Ryan, a gay male in his late twenties living in large, midwestern city, describes an incident in which he went through official channels of a company that he didn't work for to address the harassing behavior of one of its drivers. Like Natalie, whose story was recounted earlier, Ryan used the gay community as leverage.

I was driving down a two-lane street, and I was pulled into the center lane to make a left turn. I looked over and there was a guy in a delivery truck who, when the light turned green, said something along the lines of "You fucking faggot." So, that made me angry, and after a couple of cars passed me and there was a break in the traffic, I got over into his lane and followed him enough that I could get the name of the company on the truck. Then I went to a phone booth, looked up the company, and found out that it was in the area where I was. I went immediately to this place of business and talked to the woman up front.

I'm not a very confrontational person. It makes me very nervous, and I get…shaky and quaky, and my voice gets cracky. And I told this woman that one of their employees [had] made some derogatory remarks as he passed me [in his truck], and that I wanted to know what they were going do about it. At first she was sort of sensitive to me as a potential customer. But as I started talking, she got sort of defensive. And when I explained that it was an anti-gay slur, you could see that she thought, "Big deal!" But I got her to admit that it was unprofessional and inappropriate of this person and that she would talk to this person or have someone talk to this person. And I also told her that it was bashing behavior and that I was going to report it to Stonewall Union, [the local gay and lesbian organization], hoping to kind of leverage a better response by showing that it's not just one lone person, but that there's this bigger force, and that it's a bigger kind of issue here - that I'm not alone.

Using Humor

Humor has long been used to dehumanize and humiliate us. Anti-gay jokes are a homophobic staple of school, work, and play settings. In *Straight Jobs, Gay Lives,* a diversity trainer describes how he takes the power and the sting out of anti-gay jokes:

What I have found is that the surest, most effective way to just shut the whole conversation up is right after the joke is told, you just look at everybody and say quite seriously, `I don't get it.'

It embarrasses people so much when I say, `I don't get it. Was that a joke? Was that supposed to be funny? I don't' get it.' All the sudden, people stop. Nobody wants to be the one to have to explain. It's amazing, because it shuts down not only that person who told the joke but all the laughter. All of it stops. There's that pause where everybody has to think about why was that joke supposed to be so funny. And nobody has to come out.... It just cuts to the chase and it's over. And they're too embarrassed to do it again. *They're* the ones who are embarrassed.[44]

Humor isn't just a tool used against us. We can also use humor to defend ourselves. Two respondents, Sam, a gay man in his late twenties, and Jaime, a bisexual man in his mid twenties, both of whom live in large, midwestern cities, used humor to stop harassment.

Sam explains how he used a sassy comeback to a group of teenagers that harassed him outside a bar.

> There were some young kids walking on the opposite side of the street, and I left the gay bar. They didn't say anything at first, but then, as we more or less passed each other on the opposite side of the street, they started yelling. I didn't turn around. I didn't say anything. But for shits and giggles, I jumped in my car, did a u-ie, came up beside them and put down my window. They started yelling at me, "Hey, faggot, suck my dick." And I said, "Well, honey, you'd be the one sucking mine."
>
> I wasn't enraged or upset about what they said as much as I thought, "I just want to play with these kids because they are so stupid and they really think that they're upsetting me tremendously. I'm going to throw it back in their face." I got a kick out of it. I saw the situation. I wasn't putting myself in any harm. I wasn't harming anybody else.

Jaime describes how he silenced a group of male teenage harassers by using verbal confrontation, humor and the crowd.

> I was going to a professional women's basketball game. I was on the bus, and some teenagers got on, big guys, and sat next to me. We were in the back, where it's just a long seat that completely spans the back of the bus. Three of them squeezed in next to me. And then they started being really rowdy, rambunctious and rough, spilling on to me all the time and hitting me on the arm; then one of them elbowed me in the face finally. And I turned around to them and said, "Can you please cut this out. I'm getting irritated by this." And he said, "Well, hey, we paid

money too." I said, "I don't care. Cut this out now. Please. Either that or you get off the bus, and I'll complain."

So he turned around. I could almost predict what he was going to say.... And he said it really loud so everyone could hear it in order to try to shame me (I had my leather jacket and boots on). He said, "Oh, he's probably got a fucking apron on underneath those fucking cowboy clothes. Fucking faggot."

...Maybe it was because I was going to a professional women's basketball game, and I was really empowered to see them.... I turned around and I yelled out, so that the entire bus could hear, "Actually you're right. I am a faggot, and I do love to fuck, so that makes me a fucking faggot. But I don't have my apron on today. I do have my butt plug on, though, and would you like to share it with me?" The entire bus cracked up. I was laughing at myself to laugh at them, in a way, but the bus was laughing with me. The teenagers were silent and dead still the rest of the way.

Jaime explains his strategy:

My advice to anybody is that you are safest in a crowd. There's just so much they can do if you are trying to make it as public as possible. In a crowd, when I am harassed, I make it very public. I try to get everybody involved. So there's just so much they can do. Otherwise they can get away with giving you a punch or a lick here or there...

Humor isn't just a tool that we can use in public settings against strangers. Donna, a lesbian in her mid forties, describes how she has used humor to combat the slights of well meaning but ignorant acquaintances.

When I was pregnant with Chelsea, [my son, Branden's] principal asked me how I got pregnant. And I said, "Through insemination." And she said, "Well, I thought that you were married to Branden's father." And I said, "No, Branden was through insemination as well." And she said, "But he looks normal." And I said, "We've had him checked out. He's real close to being normal. You know, he's pretty much got lungs and hands, toes, feet, just like these other kids."...She said, "Oh, I guess that was a silly question." And I said, "No, that was stupid. What do you think he's going to look like?" And she said, "Well, I didn't know." I said, "Norma, sperm, egg, that's all it takes to make a real person."

In another example, Donna shows how humor can be used to challenge homophobic stereotypes.

One of the girls I work with now, she's 26.... We were all sitting around talking, and she said (sort of stuttering), "Do you think anyone here at our office is attractive?" And I looked at her and I said, "You." She was like, "Stop it." And I said, "I go home and dream about all of you girls every night. What do you think I am?" So I just sort of blow it right back to them and let them see the stupidity of it.

Personalizing harassment

Personalizing harassment is another way to put an end to obnoxious comments and behavior. This can be done by coming out to the offender(s) or by helping the offender(s) empathize with the target of harassment. Carla, a lesbian college student who worked in a small diner in a midwestern city, demonstrates the power of coming out as an option.

What started everything was the new employees who came in at the beginning of the summer. They gay-bashed constantly, using negative slurs and mocking the lifestyle, lisping and sashaying everywhere. Then they would hit on me. I was so ready to just beat the living shit out of them, but held back. After work, the two 21-year-olds were out smoking, and I walked out to them. They were being assholes again, pretending that they were gay, and I just blurted out, very matter-of-fact, "Shut up, guys.... I'm a lesbian." At first, they thought I was joking, and they said, "Well, we're gay too." And I said, "No, you don't get it. I'm a LESBIAN. A BIG ONE." They were dumbfounded. Then I continued, asking them to restrain the vocal liberties that they had been taking, remarking that they won't attract anyone with such offensive language. Now, they're a lot better, not saying "fag," etc. I mean, together, we joke about how I had to break their hearts.

While coming out can be a particularly effective way to personalize harassment, helping harassers have empathy about what it would feel like to have people act towards them the way that they behaved towards others can also do it. For example, in *Straight Jobs, Gay Lives*, Richard Stern recounts how he changed the offensive behavior of a colleague by relating anti-gay comments to anti-Semitic comments. Josh had shouted, "Pat's queer!" at Pat, a colleague who was known to be gay, while he and Richard were walking behind Pat. Later, Richard called Josh into his office to confront him. He used the fact that both he and Josh were Jewish to help make the point. He told Josh, "People who are gay don't like to be called queer.... It's as bad as someone calling you or me a kike." The confrontation worked, because not only did Josh apologize, but he also promised not to make homophobic comments in the future[45].

Exercises

Many of us face at least some form of harassment, ranging from fragments of anti-GLBT conversation like the ones that Natalie heard in the grocery store, to ignorant comments like those made by Donna's co-worker, to overtly menacing anti-GLBT comments like those directed at Ryan and Jaime. Anti-GLBT comments and harassment not only affect our safety, they often echo the self-hating themes that are woven through most of our tapestries. As a consequence, responding to anti-GLBT comments and/or harassment must occur on two levels: internally, in terms of how we let harassment affect us; and externally, in terms of how we respond to it.

At an internal level, we take the sting out of harassment by letting go of the negative messages that have been directed at us over the years and replacing them with positive ones. At an external level, we can confront harassment head-on by defining and interpreting the situation and telling the offender what to do, using clear, direct statements and using strong, serious body language. In this chapter, I went over taking the sting out of harassment and verbal confrontation. In the chapters that follow, I will cover responding to physical attacks.

Exercise 6.1: The first step in rooting out negative messages is to identify them and attribute them to their original author. So, set aside an hour, close the door, turn the ringer off your phone, and eliminate as many other distractions as you can. Get a stack of 3 x 5 index cards and the writing utensil of your choice, and sit someplace where you can comfortably write. Now, think of the negative messages that you tell yourself on a daily basis. Write down one message on each card. Under each message, write down the person or group's name that originally gave you that message and how old you were when the message was given. For example, my brother used to call me stupid all the time. Now, when I'm having a bad day, I catch myself calling myself "stupid" a lot. So, I write, "You're so stupid," put my brother's name under it, and write, "age 7-21."

It is likely that you will not remember all of the negative messages in one sitting. That's okay. Just write the new messages along with the main culprits on cards and add them to your stack. The results can be surprising and quite healing. Doing this exercise will help you to see that the negative messages in your head are not really yours. They belong to someone else and to some other time.

Exercise 6.2: Find a quiet place to sit or lay down. Eliminate as many distractions as you can by closing the door, turning off the telephone ringer, etc. Read through the following vignette and then follow the directions below.

You're standing in line at your local library. It's a wet, gloomy day, so lots of people are in the library, and the line is relatively long. When you get to the front of the line, a belligerent teenager mumbles, "Move over, faggot," as he tries to cut in front of you. You take a deep breath, hold your ground, lengthen your spine and look the boy in the eye. You tell him in a voice loud enough for other people to hear, "You're trying to intimidate me so that you can cut to the front of the line. Back off, go to the end of the line and wait like the rest of us did." Other patrons support you with their menacing stares at the attempted line-cutter. When it's your turn to step up to the checkout counter, the clerk tells you, "Way to go! Kids need to know that they can't just push us around like that." After checking out your items, you see that your harasser has slunk to the end of the line, and you walk outside to your car. Once in your car, you take few deep breaths and let yourself feel your success. You remind yourself that you just confronted someone, and you feel as though you just won your first race.

Sit or lie down and close your eyes. Take a few deep breaths, focusing on the air as it moves through your body. On your next few breaths, see if you can feel your lungs filling at the bottom, pushing your belly out. Next, see if you can expand your rib cage outward for a few breaths. Finally, see if you can breathe into your upper lungs, under your collarbone, for a few breaths. Now, put yourself in the vignette and imagine yourself confronting the harasser. (If you just can't imagine yourself doing it, try imagining a super hero doing the confrontation.) If you get frightened, remind yourself that you are imagining it, that everything is under your control, and that no one can hurt you.

CHAPTER 7
Avoiding Attacks: Why Fight If You Don't Have To?

In the last chapter, I described how to use verbal confrontation to respond to physical intimidation and verbal harassment to deter would-be attackers from escalating into violence. But verbal confrontation isn't always possible and may not be the best option even if it is possible. In this chapter, I talk about how to defend yourself by avoiding attacks altogether.

I realize that the word "avoid" seems to imply cowardice. Most of us live in a culture that celebrates violence. We are inundated with images of "good guys" and "bad guys" going to battle with their fists, feet and an arsenal of weaponry. The message that these images send is clear: heroes don't avoid fights. They hold their ground and kick ass. As we watch these scenes, we forget that they are highly choreographed and often involve as much by smoke and mirrors as skill and discount our own self-defense efforts because they are not as glamorous as what we see on screen.

Unfortunately, in the real world, attacks are not neatly choreographed and the smoke and mirrors of the screen world are noticeably absent. Even in the best-case scenario, fighting back often results in some sort of injury. At the bare minimum you risk breaking a nail. And the bottom line is that self-defense is not the same as fighting. The goal is not to defeat one's opponent. The goal of self-defense is to get away. The best defense against a physical attack is to avoid it all together. Sometimes verbal confrontation can help you do this, other times, you may need to use some avoidance techniques. Avoidance may not be as glamorous as a round kick to the head, but it is much better self-defense.

If you've ever watched a horror movie or a martial arts film, you have probably heard your gut screaming that something's about to happen long before it actually does. You see the creepy looking guy carrying a butcher knife creeping into the bathroom or the mercenary armed with an anvil creeping up on the "hero" in a warehouse. The music builds up ominously and then, bam, the intended victim is dead or the "hero" has to fight for his or her life. Often the "evil" is so obvious that it's hard to believe that the intended victim or didn't see it coming.

The build up of tension and culminating death or fight is what makes movies exciting. Few people would pay to watch someone who avoided unnecessary risks and avoided fights and/or didn't get killed because they acted on their intuition. Ironically, in real life, people are willing to pay lots of money to find out how to avoid the types of scenarios that are so exciting on film.

The good news is that we already have what it takes to avoid attacks. As discussed in Chapter 4, we are all equipped with intuition, which acts as a personal security system. This awareness or "security system" is the best tool we have to help us avoid being attacked. And, just like electronic security systems, our personal security system works pretty well when we pay attention to it. We tend to run into problems because we either forget to turn our awareness on or we ignore it when it does go off. By tuning in on your awareness, listening to your gut it when it yells out, "Hey you! Something's wrong!" and getting out of harm's way, you can avoid a lot of unnecessary pain.

Safety Tips

There are a few easy things that you can do to augment your intuition and to help yourself avoid being attacked.

Be aware of your environment. In general, well-lit, highly populated streets are safer than poorly lit, unpopulated areas such as back streets, alleys, parks, construction sites, vacant buildings and parking lots. When you are in a more isolated area, think about where you could go for help if need be. Is there a well-lit porch that seems friendly? Do you know where there is an open store, restaurant or other place of business nearby?

Be aware of your body language and your "vulnerabilities." If you are differently-abled, depressed, slinking along, looking lost, wearing shoes or other clothes that make it difficult to run, listening to a Walkman or intoxicated, you are more vulnerable and therefore look like a better target to any would-be attackers. As a consequence, you need to pay even more attention to your surroundings under these circumstances. It is also a good idea to try to avoid doing the things that make you more vulnerable in public by wearing shoes and clothes that you can move in (and run in, if need be) when out on the street and by leaving your walkman at home.

Be aware of the people that are around you. Take note of who is in front and behind you. If you feel threatened by the people around you, think about your options and take the one that's most likely to keep you safe. Often, for example, it's a good idea to cross the street, change direction, or run to a safe place if you feel threatened by someone or some group ahead, behind or beside you. If you have to maintain your course, you can watch people carefully, letting them know that you are keeping an eye on them. It's more difficult for someone to take you by surprise when you're watching them; attackers know this.

Plan ahead. If you are going someplace where you need directions, plan your route ahead of time so that you don't look lost. Even simple things can make you safer. For example, having your keys in your hands before you go out to your car or before you approach your door makes it less likely that you will have to fumble for them, and therefore makes you less vulnerable to attack. It's also a good idea to make sure that you have money for a bus, cab or phone call, just in case you unexpectedly need a ride home (or some other place that's safe).

Leaving with someone? If you meet someone at a bar, restaurant or party and decide to leave with that person, it's a good idea to introduce him or her to a friend, acquaintance, or bartender and tell them that you are leaving together so that someone sees the person that you're leaving with. By introducing your acquaintance to others, he or she loses his or her anonymity and may be less likely to do you harm. And if this person does end up doing something inappropriate, at least there will be other people to help identify and track the person down.

Think groups. When gay bashers attack us, they are not looking for a fight; they are looking for easy prey. This is why they tend to go after lone individuals rather than groups. Therefore, it's a good idea to go to and leave clubs or other high-risk places in groups. If you are going someplace alone, try to be aware of your increased risk and pay extra attention to your surroundings and intuition.

Avoiding Attack

Most of us do heed our intuition and take steps to avoid attacks on a daily basis. How many times, for example, have you crossed the street, gotten off an elevator or moved out of the way because you felt threatened? Other avoidance strategies include going into a place of business, going to more a populated area like a busy street or a crowd, and knocking on a door that looks friendly.

For example, when Marla, a cross-dresser in his[46] mid-thirties, was harassed by a group of teenage boys, rather than confronting them about their inappropriate behavior, Marla chose a very simple avoidance technique. He explains his strategy:

I was in Chicago with my wife one particular day. We had a little bit of free time and we decided to go to see the Field Museum. And I wanted to wear a skirt. So I was in male presentation: I had short hair at the time, wearing a skirt.

I dropped my wife off at the front door, and went to park at the closest parking, which happened to be at Soldier Field, across the street,....about two blocks from the front door of the Field Museum.

So I parked the car, and then I walked, through the drizzle, toward the Field Museum. There was a bus tour of teenage boys, hanging around the front, just sort of waiting for their group to be admitted, with a little bit of free time on their hands, and they thought I was the most amusing thing they'd seen in quite awhile. It was eleven o'clock in the morning, and they were seventeen (I'm assuming they weren't drunk). Several of them decided they were going to come chasing after me, and yell at the top of their lungs, "We like girls! We like girls!"

I was so tempted to tell them "I'm so glad you told me! Otherwise I wouldn't have known!" But I thought better of it. Personal safety was at issue there, and I did what any woman would have done. I kept my eyes straight ahead and I walked in a straight line for the front door. And after only following me for about one block they left me alone.

Marla avoided being attacked both by maintaining his dignity, walking towards his destination without acknowledging his harassers, and by going into the Field Museum, a busy public place. His harassers lost interest in harassing him and left him alone.

Going into a public place like a museum, store, gas station, police substation, restaurant or other place of business is often a good way to get rid of harassers because they often don't want to draw attention to themselves. In the following examples, taken from a local GLBT newspaper, GLBT people escaped their harassers by going into a public place. In the first example, a woman escapes her harassers by going into a restaurant.

A woman reported she was harassed Nov. 5 as she walked to her car after leaving a gay business downtown. The harassers, two young men, followed her and yelled sexist and ant-gay slurs. She entered a restaurant and the men fled...[47].

Similarly, two men got away from their harassers by going into a store.

> Two men reported they were followed and harassed by a group of young men in a late model white car at about 10:30 p.m. April 16 in the Short North area. The harassers reportedly used anti-gay slurs and threatening language while following them. When the two victims turned around and entered a store, the men in the car left[48].

Going to a more populated area is another tactic that often deters harassers and other would-be assailants from escalating their actions into physical violence. In the example that follows, a man eluded a group of harassers that had begun following him by returning to a busy street.

> A man reported that as he walked down a side street off High Street in the Short North on June 15 at 10:00 p.m., three young men began following him, making anti-gay threats and harassing statements. The victim crossed the street and turned back toward High Street. When he reached the busy street, the harassers went away[49].

Likewise, a lesbian couple evaded their potential attackers by going back into a crowd.

> A lesbian couple leaving the July 3 Red, White and Boom! celebration with their arms around each other were followed and verbally harassed by two white men. The victims said the perpetrators made lewd suggestions on how they could persuade the women to become heterosexual. After being followed for a block, the women circled around, heading back toward the populated fireworks area, causing the harassers to leave[50].

In the next example, a man walking his dog escaped a group of harassers by going to someone's porch.

A gay man walking his dog on Buttles Avenue alongside Goodale Park on May 15 around 11:00pm was verbally harassed by three teens shouting, "Looking for dick, faggot?" and other slurs, the victim reported. As the perpetrators got closer, the victim crossed the street and went to a lighted porch to request help. The teens ran when they saw the man go to the house...[51].

Each of these examples illustrates successful self-defense. All of the intended victims avoided what might have turned out to be a violent attack simply by getting out of harm's way.

Exercises

Though avoidance strategies tend to work very well, many people feel powerless rather than empowered when using such strategies. The feeling of powerlessness comes from focusing on the fear that led them to take evasive action rather than focusing on the fact that their strategies worked. This response is heavily shaped by the cultural message that only sissies and cowards avoid fights. The corollary to this message is that there is a very fine line between courage and stupidity. Risking one's life to prove that one is not a coward is stupid. Self-defense requires that you let go of your ego and trust your gut on how to respond to situations. If you felt threatened and avoided a fight, you defended yourself. That's something to be proud of.

In this chapter I went over avoidance strategies. In the next chapter I will go over physical techniques that you can use when avoidance and verbal confrontation are not available options. The exercises that follow should help you to get used to the idea of using avoidance strategies and to redefine situations in which you used avoidance strategies as successful.

Exercise 7.1: As you go about your routine activities in the next week, think about where you could go if you needed to get to safety quickly. Take notice of which streets are well lit and less well lit, and where stores, restaurants and other businesses are located where you could seek refuge. As you walk through residential areas, notice which houses look as though someone is home. Try to make a habit of observing your surroundings in this way.

Exercise 7.2: Think back to a time in which you avoided a situation or group of people because you felt threatened. Perhaps you got off an elevator because someone's presence just didn't feel comfortable to you. Perhaps you crossed the street to avoid having to walk through or by a group of people who seemed intimidating. Maybe you walked into a store or rang someone's doorbell because it seemed like someone was following you. As you think about that incident, instead of focusing on your fear and possible feelings of powerlessness, think about what you did right! You got out of harm's way! You avoided a physical confrontation! Pat yourself on the back for successfully defending yourself!

CHAPTER 8
Responding to Physical Threats and Assault

It's not always possible to prevent or avoid a violent encounter. Attackers sometimes get past your protective barrier, and they are not always deterred by verbal confrontation or by the possibility of other people seeing them. When this happens, physical resistance may be your best option. In the last chapter, I talked about avoidance strategies. In this chapter, I will go over some basic self-defense techniques and share stories of people who successfully defended themselves from physical threats and violence.

But won't I get hurt worse?

There is always as least one person in each self-defense class that I teach who raises this issue: "If I fight back, won't he (or she) hurt me even worse?" This is a common fear, but it's not based on reality. While there haven't been any studies specifically looking at the impact of resistance on avoiding anti-GLBT violence, there have been a number of studies on the impact of resistance in avoiding sexual assault[52]. These studies consistently show that women who used active resistance strategies such as yelling, running, and physical resistance, such as kicking or punching, were much more likely to avoid being raped than those who used more passive strategies such as cooperation, non-cooperation without resistance, making a moral appeal, crying, or reasoning[53]. In *Stopping Rape*, the most well known study on successful survival strategies, Pauline Bart and Patricia O'Brian[54] found:

* 81% of women who fled or tried to flee avoided rape
* 75% of women who physically resisted avoided rape
* 63% of women who screamed or yelled avoided rape

* 54% of women who used cognitive verbal techniques (i.e. reasoning with or trying to con the attacker or attempting to make attacker see her as a human being) avoided rape
* 44% of women who used pleading avoided rape
* 0% of women who made no attempt to resist avoided rape.

In addition, Bart and O'Brian found no relationship between a woman's use of physical resistance and an attacker's use of additional force.

Despite the lack of research on resistance to anti-GLBT violence, it is reasonable to assume that fighting back will improve one's chances of getting away unharmed or at least with less injury. Like rapists, gay-bashers don't expect their victims to make a scene, fight back, or even to report the offense. That's part of the reason they go after us. Since our attackers don't expect us to resist, our resistance comes as a surprise and throws them off. Therefore, resisting an attack by running, yelling, punching or kicking should significantly improve your chances of getting away[55].

It's important to note that the data that we do have indicate that anti-GLBT attacks, especially against men presumed to be gay, are more likely to involve multiple assailants, are more likely to occur in public settings, are more likely to involve strangers, and are more likely to involve weapons than sexual assaults against women. However, this gendered pattern of anti-gay violence is similar to the gendered patterns of regular offenses. Men are more likely to be attacked in public by strangers, while women are more likely to be attacked in private settings by someone they know.

Two Rules. There are only two rules in self-defense. Rule number one: Do not go anywhere with an assailant, even if he or she has a weapon. The only reason that an assailant would want you to change locations is to make you more vulnerable, reduce your chances of escape and lower their risk of getting caught. If an assailant is going to kill you, he or she is more likely to do so in a secluded area than outside a bar. Run, yell, pretend to faint, go limp, or simply refuse to go—whatever it takes—but don't go with the assailant. Rule number two: Never let an assailant tie you up. Again, the point of this is to make you more vulnerable, less able to fight back and less able to escape.

Beyond rules and statistics, the bottom line is that you must trust your gut. Knowing how to run, kick, punch and yell increases your options. If your gut is telling you, "Run as fast and as far as possible," then you should run. If your gut is telling you that it's time to lay low and be quiet, then that's what you should do. The trick is learning to distinguish the voice of panic from the voice of your gut. Like everything else, this takes breathing and practice.

Physical Self-Defense Techniques

The research that has been done on avoiding assault is pretty clear that running, yelling, and kicking or punching are the best defenses against attack. I am going to present a few of the most basic self-defense techniques. A full discussion of techniques is beyond the scope of this book. Remember that the options presented here are among many options available to you; you may choose not to use them. If you have been attacked before and didn't use any physical self-defense, be easy on yourself. You did the best that you could at the time.

You do not necessarily need to take a self-defense class in order to use these techniques, but I strongly recommend that you do if you can find one in your area. Being in a class allows you to process your feelings and practice your skills in a supportive setting. If you can't take a class, it would be very helpful to practice these techniques with a supportive friend[56].

If you have been attacked or raped before, you may find these techniques to be emotionally difficult. It is important to find a way to work through that difficulty and to practice so that if an incident happens, you will be more prepared. Practicing also may help you to break through the wall of fear that many survivors live behind.

Running and yelling

Running is usually your best option if you are able to do that. Remember that the point of self-defense is always to get away unharmed (or with the least possible injury to oneself). If you can run, run. Before you do anything, however, assess the situation. Check out your surroundings. Can you run towards a busy space, such as a street or sidewalk? Is there an exit that you can see, or an entrance into a building like a big store with security or at least people? You may get winded and you may break a sweat, but if you can get away, you won't get hit. And remember that you will increase your odds of getting away if you yell while you run.

Yelling is very simple, but most people need some coaching on it. (I actually enrolled in a self-defense class because I realized that I couldn't yell. Some of it was physical; I didn't know how to yell in a way that didn't hurt my vocal chords. But mostly I was terrified to make a scene.) Attackers count on our silence, so it's a good idea to warm up to the idea of making a scene.

In order to yell most effectively, you need to yell from the diaphragm. If you were in band, choir or drama club in high school, you may remember how to use your diaphragm effectively in order to sing, play a woodwind or brass instrument, or project your voice from the stage. In order to get a feel for this, take a deep breath—one that expands your belly - relax your throat, and use that breath and your diaphragm to yell. This should not hurt your vocal chords. If it does, you either are not yelling from your diaphragm or you are tensing your throat. Try again until you get it. Driving in the car with the windows rolled up is my favorite place to practice this yell. People probably just think I'm singing, and I don't worry about the neighbors getting frightened or annoyed.

Running Away

The following examples show how running can help to avoid an attack or at to least minimize the damage. In the first example, Mark, a gay white male in his late twenties, successfully escaped a potential gay bashing. Mark, his partner and a couple of friends heard a group of kids making anti-gay remarks when they were walking through their neighborhood in a large, Midwestern city. A little bit later, Mark remembered that he had left something in his car and went to get it.

> When I got out of my car, this little, probably ten-year-old, girl started screaming at me, "You called my brother this, [some sort of epithet]." I just said, "No, I don't even know you…whatever." And she made the comment, "Well, my brother can whip your ass." I just ignored it and started walking to my house, and [the brother] started chasing me. And I made it to the door just before he did, [and] slammed the door. He was banging on the door. I thought, "Oh well, it will go away, no big deal." Probably an hour later, (we didn't have air conditioning) we opened the door, screen door locked, thinking, "No big deal, they're gone. They live on another street anyway, around the corner." And it probably wasn't five minutes later that a huge landscaping timber out of our flowerbed came through the screen door, into the living room where we were sitting. So, we looked out, saw it was them. Then we looked out the back window, saw that they were going towards their house.

By running into his house and slamming his door behind him, Mark avoided what probably would have turned out to be a physical confrontation. Running can also be a useful strategy once an attack has already begun. In this example from a Midwestern regional GLBT paper, a woman ran to escape further attack.

> A 19-year-old woman reported that she was physically assaulted by two white men in their early 20's on October 17 at 10:00pm in Italian Village. The two men allegedly punched her and pushed her to the ground, verbally harassing her with statements like, "You think you're tough, dyke?" throughout. The woman broke free and ran to a busy intersection; her assailants did not follow. The victim suffered bruises and a loose tooth[57].

Punching and Kicking

Stance is the next basic thing that you need to work on. In order to make your punches and kicks effective, you need to have your weight balanced. The best and easiest way to do this is to get into a martial arts or boxer stance with one foot in front of the other and your feet shoulder width apart. Your knees should be slightly bent, and you should feel solid with the ground so that if someone were to push you, you wouldn't lose your balance. In "neutral" position, your hands should be out of your pockets, hanging loosely at your sides. If you have your hands in your pockets or your arms folded, it will take you more time to get them untangled so that you can use them if you need them. It's a good idea to practice hanging your hands at your side. Any time that you catch yourself putting them in your pockets or folding them, shake them out and hang them back at your sides.

You also might have someone test your stance by pushing you a little. (They should not try to push you over as if you were a tackle dummy.) If your balance is good, have them push a little harder. If it's still good, you're in good shape. If you lose your balance and start to wobble over, adjust your stance. Make sure that your feet are a little wider than shoulder width apart and have then try again. If you still wobble, bring your front foot back a little. At the first sign of trouble, it's a good idea to bring your hands up to waist or chest level so that you can quickly block or execute a punch if need be.

Punching is probably what you think of when you think about self-defense. If you are going to punch with your fist, you need to make sure that you make a nice, tight fist, with your thumb wrapped around the outside. Using your fist is fine, but using your palm heel to strike with is better because it's padded and won't hurt you as much. Boxers wear gloves to protect their hands. They actually give boxers more power because they can hit surfaces like the side of the head that they can't hit without gloves without the risk of breaking their fingers.

The palm heel strike uses the heel of the palm, the padded area on the palm side of your hand below your pinky that connects to your wrist. To make a palm heel, curl your fingers, bend your wrist back (as in "Talk to the hand" or like a police officer does when she or he makes the sign for "Stop"—except that your fingers are curled down) and bring your thumb in so that it touches the side of your hand. Make sure that your fingers are pulled back tightly so that you don't risk breaking them.

Next, you need to know how to punch. The first step of any punch is to get into a balanced position like the stance described above. The easiest way to punch is to get your hands in "boxing" position, with your hands up near your nose and your elbows tucked in. This puts your hands in a good position to block punches and protect your head. Your lead hand (the hand corresponding to the foot you have in front) should be in front. The trick to a good punch is that you must use your whole body. Hips are where your power is, so throw the punch from your hips. Your hips should move with the punch, so that when you extend your arm, the movement is coming from your hip.

You can punch with either the lead or rear hand, but lead hand has much less power than the rear hand. For some people, punching with both hands will take practice. If you feel yourself losing balance when you punch with either your lead or your rear hand, slow down and look at what you're doing. It's very likely that you are trying to punch outside your range. A way to correct this is to stand facing a wall at an arm's length distance. Your fist or palm heel should be able to touch the wall only when your shoulders are exactly square to the wall. (Your shoulders aren't square in the stance.) Now, slowly and gently (and I do mean slowly and gently) punch the wall. You are training your body technique and distance right now; you can add speed and power later.

Another common mistake that people make is to tense their muscles while they punch. Somehow they think that they are hitting harder because they are working harder. Unfortunately, this is not the case. It's like putting your brakes on and trying to speed down the highway. You can still drive with the brakes on and your car is working harder to go the same distance, but it's certainly not more effective. So, if you're still close to the wall, back away a bit. Take a deep breath, let all that tension out of your arms and shoulders (you can keep the tension in your fist or your palm heel), and punch in slow motion 10 times with each hand. You should feel your hand gliding to and away from you like silk. Now, punch 10 times with each hand quickly. Your punches should still feel like silk as they glide.

Remember, if you are striking with a heel palm, make sure that you bring your thumb close to your hand and pull your fingers back and strike with the bottom outside portion of your palm. If you are using a fist, make sure your fingers are tightly tucked in and your thumb is out, wrapped around your fingers. You can punch someone in the nose, the throat, or the jaw with your fist. With your heel palm, you can strike someone on the nose, under the chin, or in the crotch.

Kicking. If you think that the best sorts of kicks to use to defend yourself are the flying kicks and the kicks to the head seen martial arts films, you need to think again. Those fancy kicks look great on film, but in reality they take a lot more skill and practice and pack less power than low kicks. The best self-defense kicks, unless you are a very skilled martial artist, are low kicks. Low kicks give you more "bang for your buck." By stomping someone's foot and breaking it, you are just as effective at disabling the person as you are by kicking the person in the hip and breaking the hipbone. And it's a lot easier to break someone's foot than it is to break someone's hip.

Kicks aren't as complicated as most people think that they are. If you can walk up stairs, you can kick. You can kick with either foot, but it's easier to kick with the rear leg, so practice first kicking with your rear leg. All kicks start with this basic movement. Get into your stance. Lift your knee, like you are going up stairs, and bring your calf up to your thigh (this is chambering your kick); then shoot your foot out from your knee.

There are a number of types of kicks, but I'm only going to cover the most basic two: the front kick and the stomp kick. The **front kick** gives you several target options. You can kick the attacker in the groin, the knee, or the inner thigh. To kick the groin: chamber your leg, point your toes and hit the groin with your shin. If you are aiming for the knee or the inner thigh, chamber your leg, curl your toes back and hit the target (the knee or inner thigh) with the ball of your foot. It is a good idea to find something, a wall, a punching bag, or a chair, that you can use to slowly and gently kick to practice your distance.

The **stomp kick** is an excellent kick if your attacker is on the ground or you want to aim for the top of the attacker's foot or ankle. To execute the kick, chamber your leg and just stomp like you are stomping a cockroach with your heel.

Responding to Physical Attacks

In the examples that follow, GLBT people use a variety of techniques to avoid or minimize a violent attack. I just want to point out a few things to think about as you read through these scenarios. First, self-defense is not algebraic; a + b doesn't necessarily equal c. What I mean by this is that there are no set strategies for various attacks. Every situation is different. You will choose the best option for you at the time. I tried to include a variety of scenarios to help you see that there are a variety of options.

Second, the point of self-defense is to get out of a situation with as little harm to yourself as possible. This is an important consideration to keep in mind as you review your own self-defense experiences and read through the following examples. The scenarios are organized along a continuum of both strategy and assumed risk.

The next two examples show how would-be victims stopped attacks by punching their attackers. In the first example, taken from the local GLBT newspaper, a self-defense course graduate put his training to use to put an end to a local gay-basher's "career."

> He finally confronted one of his victims face-to-face, and what did it get him? A bloody nose and a court date. On September 26 at about 5:30pm, a man in a brown van chased a gay male driving down Central Avenue, weaving through traffic and yelling anti-gay comments like, "Get off the road, faggot!" The perpetrator and his vehicle fit the description of a man in a brown van who [had] reportedly harassed several other gay, lesbian and bisexual drivers in separate incidents in late spring and summer. In each case, the driver identified a gay-owned car by stickers or other gay-related insignia and screamed threats and obscenities at them while following them through the streets. In the September 26 incident, the victim pulled into a store parking lot in an attempt to get into a public area to dissuade the assailant. As the victim was walking toward the

store, the assailant got out of the van, came up to the assailant and shoved him on the shoulder.

He didn't get the reaction he wanted. The victim - a graduate of a BRAVO self-defense training - punched the perpetrator in the face, bloodying his nose and forcing him to the ground. After he'd been hit, the assailant reportedly said, "You faggots aren't supposed to fight back." Police were called, witnesses confirmed the victim's report, and the man was arrested for assault. He may also be charged with ethnic intimidation, and if his license plates match those from prior reports, could face additional charges from the earlier incidents[58].

We live in a culture that teaches men that in order to be real men, they must have sex with women. If a woman doesn't concede to sex willingly, some men interpret this maxim to mean that it's okay, and possibly even necessary, to use force to get what they want. This behavior constitutes rape. Lesbians and bisexual women often are the targets of would-be rapists not only because they are women, but because attackers want to punish these women for not being straight or want to make them straight. Gay and bi-sexual men also are targeted for rape for similar reasons.

In the following example, Kelly, a lesbian high school student, stymies a classmate's plan to rape her.

I was 15, out with a male the same age. He was on the football team, and had asked for help on a paper. I was the good English student, willing to help him, and afterwards he took me to a movie to thank me for all the help. Things were pleasant until after the movie. We were waiting in front of the movie theater for his parents to pick us up, and when they were late, we went on a walk to get some ice cream. That's when I had to fight him.

I learned later that he told his folks to pick us up an hour later than when the movie first got out (he told his father that it was a "date," and to give us some "alone time"). He did this because he had heard rumors about me, and wanted to see how "true" they were, if I really was "a fucking dyke...."

We went out for a walk after ice cream, sitting out under the stars in a field next to the theater, looking out for his parents' car. He started to kiss me, and I freaked out, I stood up.... But he didn't get up. I went to pull him up by his arm, telling him that I thought I saw his parents and that we should go back, but instead, he pulled me down and climbed onto me to rape me. I remember that he was laughing a bit at first, saying things like "come on, let's show them that you're a real woman," etc. Ugh. I was trying to push him off, but he got more forceful, and I then decked him a good one, right on the nose. Blood all over his face and hands.... Told him, "no." I just laid there, catching my breath, and he was just sitting between my spread legs, crying. After a few moments, I got up, and looked down on him, and said, "Now stop acting like a fucking asshole and walk me back to the theater like a goddamned gentleman."

Beyond Punching and Kicking

In the past two examples, potential victims used punching to either avoid an attack or to stop an attack from escalating. In the next two examples, Jaime, a bisexual graduate student in his mid-twenties, uses his intuition as well as physical, mental and verbal techniques to defend himself against multiple attackers. Both of his stories demonstrate that you don't always have to fight back physically to defend yourself.

In the first example, street harassment unexpectedly escalates to violence. The incident actually started before Jaime arrived at the scene. He was waiting at a different corner for his partner so that they could go to their car. A block or two down from him, a group of college-aged people was selling magazine subscriptions on the corner across the street from the university. When his partner, Dehlia, walked by, they harassed her.

Jaime explains, "They were very vocal, very "in your face…." I'd seen them before and I'd seen them really go after people, and if someone said no, they would really come down. They would use all kinds of epithets, many of them being queer-related. "You faggot." "You dyke." "These sports magazines scare you off."

Dehlia was very intimidated by the harassment, and instead of going to meet Jaime, she went to the house of Laney, a friend. Laney and Dehlia then drove back to where the harassers were. Jaime continues:

> Meanwhile, I'm still waiting for my partner on the corner. I had no idea what was happening. So I started walking. And at the same time…[the harassers] were accosting this person right in front of me. "You faggot. Why aren't you buying something?" It was just totally out of control. So I went up to them and said, "What is your problem? Why are you doing this?" And there was only one person there at the time. I didn't realize that there was a network of people spread all over, all within visual distance.

> At that moment, a car screeched to a halt in front of me…and Dehlia and Laney were in the car.

> So the guy catches hold of my hair immediately. And Laney said, "You have two seconds, buddy, let go!" And the guy looks at her and then whistles, and before we know it, there are five people surrounding us….

> So my first reaction was to guard my back. So I immediately put my back to the wall. We were two, Laney and me, and 5 or 6 of them…. I was trying to delay the situation as much as possible before it got physical. So I was saying anything. "I'm a cop and I'm going to arrest you." That threw him off. I was trying to delay things so that people would come to our assistance. So I

was like, "give me your ID." Totally bluffing. My whole point was to maneuver, to be the person on the offensive.... And I had my hand in my pocket as if to bring out some sort of gun and I'm shouting at them.... And then one of them said, "You're a fucking faggot, that's all you are," and immediately my second reaction was, "You are exactly right. Pull down your pants I will suck you off right now, right here."

He didn't know what to say at that point. That gave us five more seconds.... Laney was shouting at one of them.... She had her back to the street. Someone went around her and knocked her down, on the head, actually fractured her skull.... and as soon as she got knocked down, all of them turned on me.

I could see what was happening.... So I covered my head and I bent down. All this time I started taunting them. By this time, I knew they were going to hit me and I was going to get hit.... [But] I wanted to know in my head that I wasn't the one victimized, so I continued to laugh and taunt. And they couldn't really do much. I just protected my head and bent down, and took blows and I was fine. They were scared at this point because they had already knocked another person down and bought some useful seconds, and people were screaming, "Call the police! Call the police!" And then they [the perpetrators] ran.

Situations involving multiple attackers can be extremely dangerous and terrifying. Rather than freezing up or letting his anger control his actions, Jaime assessed the situation and took actions to minimize his risk of getting badly hurt. Throughout the incident Jaime made active choices. He chose to confront the magazine salesperson. Then, when he realized that there was a gang of attackers, he chose to get his back to the wall so that no one could get behind him. He also anticipated that the crowd that he was in would not tolerate this sort of violence and made a choice to use them for protection. Next, he chose to use verbal techniques to "buy time." Finally, even though they were hitting him, he chose to verbally defend himself to maintain his sense of control over the situation. Because he refused to give them his power, he felt successful. He was writing his own script rather than simply playing out the loose script that the attackers had in mind.

In another situation, Jamie was attacked outside a queer bar in New York City. He describes how he used his intuition and verbal skills to de-escalate the attack and to minimize the emotional impact of the attack.

> I've gotten beaten up in an alley in New York City after coming out of a queer club.... At first I thought it was some kind of a mugging. It wasn't. And I knew I was going to get beaten up. The thought crossed my mind that they might kill me. Even at that point, I just didn't want to give up the power. And I started [asking them], "Oh well, what are you going to do, beat me up? Nice manly men like you? Seven of you, versus one of me. Oh, let me guess, you're gonna take out a knife after some time because you feel sooo mad at me and you're gonna try and stab me, right? Ok, go ahead. Prove to yourself. Prove to your fellow people that you are sooo brave, you are such dicks." And they beat me up.

> I was pretty sure that they were going to use at least some weapon to beat up on me, but they didn't do anything. They just kicked me around a little bit.... I wasn't hurting that much, but I pretended that I was really hurt because that's what they wanted to see. And they left. And once the beating started, I just gave them what they wanted—quickly—so that they didn't actually have to go into me for any length of time....

> There were bruises and I had a cracked rib, but I was fine after some months.

Jaime's actions were successful because they served to minimize a potentially life threatening situation. I have talked a number of people who took similar evasive action but didn't define their experience as successful. I asked Jaime what he did to help himself feel successful. He explains:

> The way I think about it is, people are going to try and use their power over you in numbers, physical power...and really what they're trying to do is making themselves feel good, by making you feel bad.... So that's in my control, I figure. If I'm not going to be feeling bad by anything that they say....

"You faggot!"

"Damn, yeah! I am."

"You want to suck me?"

"Absolutely, right now, right here."

"You want to get beaten up?"

"I want to get beaten up. I enjoy it. I'm an S&M guy."

> ...[Saying] things like that almost takes the power away from them, into my hands. And after I get beaten up, I know I've done something to survive it...and to be powerful in the end.

> ...During the situation, I am scared shitless. And I really have thought a lot about what I would do in these situations.... These situations can happen any time. And I don't live in fear, but it has helped to think about what I'm gonna do.

Jaime's response highlights some important facts about self-defense and life in general. First, you can't control someone else's behavior; you can only control your own. So in following Jaime's example, it's important that when you rehash an incident in your mind, you focus only on the positive steps you took and don't worry about what the attackers might have done. Rather than beating yourself up, be gentle and remind yourself that you did the best you could with the options that you saw at the time. Second, as discussed in Chapter 6, it's important to reject the negative labels that attackers try to stick on you. By using stereotypes defensively, Jaime not only kept his power, but he also threw his attackers off balance, perhaps because he did the unexpected. Gaybashers expect you to wilt at the utterance of an anti-GLBT word. Don't give them that power over you. Third, like Jaime, it's important to rehearse situations in your mind. Think about what you might do if someone tried to attack you on the street or in your house. You might as well go through all the options. Be sure that you find a way to overcome the situation in your mind.

Exercises

You may not always be able to prevent or avoid a violent encounter. While it is scary to think about, research suggests that rather than making things worse, fighting back will improve your chances of surviving an attack. Using one simple technique such as running, yelling, punching or kicking can increase your odds of getting away. If you use two or more techniques (i.e. running and yelling or yelling and kicking), you increase your odds of success even more. Just be intentional about whatever self-defense option you chose to use. If you're going to yell, yell like you mean it. If you're going to punch, punch with every cell of your body. Don't hold anything back.

In this chapter, I went over some very basic self-defense techniques and provided some examples of how these techniques have and haven't been used. In the next chapter, I will talk about situations where active physical resistance doesn't seem like the best option.

The exercises that follow should help you get more comfortable with using your physical techniques as well as help you reduce some of the fear you have about being hit.

Exercise 8.1: Set aside 30 minutes a day for the next week and practice yelling, punching and kicking. If you have someone you can practice with, this is even better. As you practice, be gentle with yourself. Start slowly and add speed when you feel comfortable with slow motion. The point is to work on your technique. When you are practicing with a partner, do not exchange full force blows.

Exercise 8.2: As you're out and about this week, be it at the grocery store, the library, or the office, start to notice people's bodies. Don't just size them up based on their sexual allure; look at them from the perspective of where they are vulnerable. Notice their eyes, nose, throat, groin, knees, ankles and the tops of their feet. Then think what you might do, where you might strike or kick them, if they were to attack you. If you feel intimidated by someone, just remind yourself that they are not invincible. They have vulnerabilities just like you do.

Exercise 8.3: Visualization: Read through the following vignette; then follow the instructions below.

Imagine that you are leaving a large festival. Someone starts walking too closely behind you, considering that there's room for him to be walking further back. You turn around to see who it is and he calls you a dyke/faggot and starts to push you. You take a deep breath, get into your stance, yell a very loud "No!" and deliver a palm heel strike to his nose. Immediately he grabs his nose and bends over. Someone in the crowd asks if you are all right. You check in with yourself and realize that you're fine, and thank the person for asking. You feel the adrenaline flowing through your body, but you feel good because you got away. You make it back to your house without further incident.

Now, find a quiet spot where you won't be disturbed for a few minutes. Either sit or lay down and begin focusing on your breathing. Counting your breaths on the exhale is another good way to focus on your breathing. If you lose your count, start over. Otherwise, count to 21 and then start over. After you have done this for several minutes (say three or four rounds of 21 breaths), begin to play the vignette in your mind. Give yourself time to really see yourself in your mind. (If you have trouble visualizing yourself fighting back, try visualizing yourself as if you were confident and strong. If that doesn't work, try visualizing yourself as a super hero.) Make sure that you see yourself as strong and victorious. It's all happening in your mind; you have the power to control it now.

CHAPTER 9
Passive Resistance: Choosing Not to Fight Back

The last few chapters have focused on active resistance strategies: verbal confrontation, avoidance, and physically fighting back. This chapter focuses on passive resistance strategies. As discussed in Chapter Eight, using active strategies helps you to increase your odds of getting away unscathed or with minimal damage to yourself. However, there are situations in which active resistance is not the best option. At a theoretical level, it's useful to know that the odds are in your favor if you actively resist. But in any given situation, it's more important to base your reactions on your intuition. Always trust your gut!

Passive resistance is probably the most difficult self-defense concept to grasp. In our culture, passive responses are associated with passivity, which is associated with powerlessness. But passive resistance isn't simply a powerless response. It involves an active choice to not fight back based on an assessment of all the possible options (and there always is more than one option). By exploring all possible options and deciding which is the one that's going to result in the least amount of damage, you can retain your sense of power and control. By passively resisting, you are not simply submitting to someone else's plan. You are making active decisions about how to best protect yourself. The key is to consciously make a choice.

The examples that follow may be emotionally difficult to read, especially if you have been sexually assaulted or abused in the past. If you find yourself panicking or feeling emotionally overwhelmed either during or after reading this chapter, it might help to call a supportive friend or your local rape crisis helpline. (You can reach the rape crisis helpline nearest you by dialing the Rape Abuse Incest National Network (RAINN) at 1-800-656-HOPE. In addition, a list of anti-GLBT violence centers is listed in Appendix A.

You also may find yourself tempted to second guess the choices made by the men in the examples by thinking things like, "Why didn't he…?" "Why did he…?" Or "I would have…." This is a way of blaming the victim and taking the blame off the perpetrator(s). Try not to do this. Second guessing often involves setting yourself up to have a false sense of security. You are, in essence, telling yourself that if you do all the right things, nothing bad will happen to you since bad things only happen to people who do something wrong. This is a very dangerous myth. No one deserves to be assaulted, raped or hurt in any way. And no one can make someone else hurt him or her. So rather than blaming the victim, accept that the men in both situations trusted their intuition and followed the best option available to them at the time. And remember that both men lived to tell their stories. They obviously did something very right.

Passive Resistance as an Active Strategy

There always is more than one option in any situation. The problem is that sometimes all the options are pretty rotten. In these situations, it is especially important to choose consciously how you will respond. This will allow you to feel more powerful during and after the incident. This is especially important because it's important to remain fluid during an incident. Passively resisting may be the best option during one part of the attack, but your intuition may push you to respond actively seconds or minutes later.

In the first example, excerpted from "Male on Male Rape,[59]" Michael[60] describes how he made a choice to be raped rather than to face potentially more threatening anti-GLBT violence. Michael and his roommate, Tom, both gay, had been the targets of a vicious anti-GLBT harassment campaign by the other 30 men that lived on the floor of their dorm. What began as sneers and stares soon escalated to verbal abuse, menacing and death threats. Eventually, the university determined that Michael and Tom faced so much risk of being bashed or killed by their floor mates that they evacuated the entire floor, moving Michael and Tom to a hotel and splitting up the other thirty men and relocating them across campus. The university even hired armed security guards to escort Michael and Tom around campus to ensure their safety. It was in this homophobic context that Michael was raped.

Tom had gone home for the weekend, leaving Michael to deal with his homophobic neighbors alone. Michael went out to a gay dance bar, hoping to meet up with friends. While at the bar, Michael met someone, and they went to Michael's dorm room to escape the loud music, crowd and cigarette smoke. Once in the dorm room, they began to kiss. Then the man tried to unzip Michael's jeans. When Michael resisted, the man became more forceful.

> ...The more I pushed his hands away, the more aggressive he became until finally he used force. I asked him to stop, but was too embarrassed to raise my voice for fear that others next door or outside in the hallway would hear what was happening. I was afraid the men who hated me for being gay would use this situation as one more excuse to bash me. After several attempts to unfasten my jeans, he finally succeeded and yanked down my pants and underwear.

What happened next is all too predictable. The man raped Michael and then left without saying a word.

It's important to remember that Michael chose not to yell for help or physically resist because he did not want to attract even more attention to himself than his floormates had already given him. He chose to be raped rather than face further humiliation and possible violence from his neighbors.

Jaime, who recounted several incidents in Chapter Eight, similarly describes an event in which he chose to be raped rather than face even worse consequences.

> This one happened when I was in the army. I was taking a shower and this guy came up from behind me and raped me. I never turned around to look at him. It was like I knew that if I looked at him he would have to kill me. I think not looking saved my life. There were several incidents of gay men killed in the showers. I think they were raped, but no one looked into it. They covered it up.

In this situation, Jaime's gut instinct was that if even so much as turned around and looked at his perpetrator, he would be killed, so he chose to submit. By doing so, he may have saved his life.

Even though both of these examples resulted in rape, it is important to remember that not all attempted rapes result in a completed rape. For example, recall that Kelly, a lesbian high school student, stopped a classmate's attempt to rape her by punching him in the nose.

Exercises

While the odds are in your favor to actively resist an attack, fighting back is not always the best option. It's important to stay tuned in to your intuition and respond to situations accordingly. In each of the two cases recounted in this chapter, passive resistance, while resulting in rape, was what each man felt was the best survival strategy at the time.

In this chapter, I went over passive resistance strategies and the importance of exploring your options and making conscious decisions based on your gut reaction. In the next chapter I will go over weapons, both how they are used against us and how we can use weapons to defend ourselves.

The exercises that follow are designed to help people who have been raped or assaulted in the past to reframe their situation and to let go of their self-blame and sense of powerlessness.

Exercise 9.1: If reading through this chapter was emotionally triggering for you, it might be a good idea to "ground" yourself back in the present. If you are not physically safe, please call 911 or do what you need to do to get safe now! Otherwise, start by focusing on your body. If you are sitting down, feel your legs and bottom as they rest against the chair or whatever you are sitting on. If you are standing, feel your feet making contact with the floor. Take a few breaths in and out, and feel what the breath feels like in your body. Remind yourself that you are safe, and that the incident that you are remembering happened in the past and cannot hurt you now. Now, ask yourself, "What it would feel like to feel safe?" and let yourself imagine your answer. If you can't imagine what it would feel like for you to feel safe, try imagining what it would feel like for someone else to feel safe. Then let yourself feel that other person's safety.

Exercise 9.2: If you have been assaulted or raped, it can be extremely tempting to focus on what you have done "wrong" and to blame yourself for what happened to you, especially if you did not actively resist. It is not uncommon for survivors of violence or other abuse to replay the incident over and over in their minds, focusing on what they "could have" or "should have" done. This is often the case if the survivors were drunk, high, or otherwise intoxicated at the time.

This way of looking at your experience is not helpful. Try to stop doing it. Instead, look at your actions in a positive light. Remind yourself that you did the best that you could under the circumstances. If you are reading this, you survived. Obviously you did something right. If you feel that you made a mistake, perhaps because you were drunk or high, be gentle with yourself. Remind yourself that you made a mistake but that you didn't deserve what happened to you, nor did you make the person or persons hurt you. Blame them for what happened, not your self.

CHAPTER 10
Weapons

For most of us, weapons are the stuff of nightmares. We imbue weapons, especially knives and guns, with almost magical qualities, and thus feel powerless to defend ourselves against them. The media exacerbates our fear of weapons. We watch characters in movies and TV shows die instant tragic deaths after being shot, stabbed or bludgeoned. We see bullet-ridden crime scenes as dead bodies are rolled away on the evening news and read grisly accounts of murder in the newspaper.

These media images create an exaggerated sense of danger from weapons. While attacks with weapons tend to be more dangerous and cause more damage than simple physical assault, statistics from the Justice Department and the National Coalition of Anti-Violence Projects (NCAVP) indicate that most attacks do not involve weapons. Even when weapons are used, chances of surviving are pretty good.

At the same time, because weapons tend to cause more damage with less effort than simply striking someone, we can improve our defensive capabilities by wielding weapons to defend ourselves. The second half of this chapter describes how to use ordinary objects in your home and work environment as weapons and helps you rank the weapons you have available.

Survival Estimates

Bureau of Justice Statistics (BJS) do not bear out pop cultural beliefs about weapons. Data from the BJS's National Crime Victimization Survey (NCVS) and the FBI Crime Reporting Program's Supplemental Homicide Report (SHR) indicate that weapons were not involved in most violent attacks. Offenders were armed only in 34% of attacks against men and in 24% of attacks against women[61].

Data from the National Coalition of Anti-Violence Programs (NCAVP) reinforce BJS findings[62]. According to NCAVP data, only 31% in 1999 and 34%[63] in 2000 of all assaults and attempted assaults involved a weapon of any sort[64]. (See table 10.1.)

Table 10.1

Weapons involved in anti-GLBT incidents in 1999 and 2000

	1999	2000
Homicide	28	16
Total assaults and attempted assaults	726	786
Total weapons*	223	264
%**	31%	34%
Blunt objects	65	67
%	8%	9%
Projectiles	40	61
%	6%	8%
Firearms	41	25
%	6%	3%
Kinves/sharp objects	63	78
%	9%	10%
Rope/restraints	1	3
%	.1%	.4%
Vehicles	13	30
%	2%	4%

*Total assaults and attempted assaults reported that involved any sort of weapon
**Percent of all assaults/attempted assaults that involved weapons

In addition, some weapons are more dangerous than others. According to the NCAVP, incidents involving projectiles such as bottles, rocks, bricks and other thrown objects or vehicles tended to be "fleeting, launched from a distance, and less effective at causing harm to subjects.[65]" Thrown objects accounted for 6% of incidents in 1999 and 8% in 2000, and vehicles accounted for 2% of incidents in 1999 and 4% in 2000. Guns, knives and blunt objects are more dangerous. Only 6% of all assaults and attempted assaults involved firearms in 1999 and 3% in 2000, and only 9% and 10%, respectively, involved knives and other sharp objects. An additional 8% in 1999 and 9% in 2000 involved blunt objects. Taken together, these data indicate that your odds of being attacked with a weapon are fairly low.

Even if you are shot, at least with a handgun, your chances of survival are pretty good. Studies conducted by the New York Police Department suggest that if you are shot with a gun at close combat distance, you have a 75% chance of survival. According to these studies, a deliberately inflicted handgun wound will result in death only one time in four[66]. Shotguns and high-powered rifles are more dangerous. A deliberately caused wound at close range with a shotgun or high-powered rifle is almost certain to cause death[67].

Chances of surviving a knife attack are also pretty good. Our skeletal system protects our vital organs by making it difficult to stab through the skull and rib cage. As a consequence, the brain, heart and lungs are pretty safe from knife injuries. In addition, few people in our culture are skilled at fighting with knives. Unless the attacker slices through a major artery or hits an organ like the kidney, chances of surviving a knife attack are good. People have been stabbed and sliced multiple times and survived.

The NCAVP data offers further reason for optimism about the chance of surviving an attack. While one anti-GLBT homicide is too many, when looked at probabilistically, these data indicate that your overall risk of being killed in any sort of assault or attempted assault, with or without a weapon, is quite low. In 1999, based on NCAVP reported data, the odds of an assault or attempted assault resulting in death were 3.7 percent. In 2000, these odds were 2 percent[68].

Defending Against Weapons

While statistics suggest that most assaults do not involve weapons and that chances of surviving an armed attack are far better than you might expect, weapons are still dangerous. I strongly recommend taking a self-defense course to work on your weapons defense skills. A full-blown discussion on defense against weapons is beyond the scope of this book. Nonetheless, here are a few simple techniques that might be useful in the event that an armed assailant attacks you. Please note that these are just options. In the event that you actually are assaulted, the best thing that you can do is to follow your instincts.

The maxim, "Don't fight if you can run" is true especially when it comes to responding to armed assailants. If your attacker has a knife, broken beer bottle or other sharp weapon, and you think that you can get away, run to a safe place. If not, try to keep something—a purse, backpack, bag, or coat—between you and the weapon, so that if the attacker stabs or slices at you, the attacker hits your "shield" rather than your body. You still can fight back, but you have to be careful to avoid getting badly cut.

If an attacker grabs you with one hand while he or she has a knife in the other, it is even more important to put something between you and the knife, even if you have to hold the blade with your fingers. You can still punch and kick the attacker in an effort to get away. Stomp kicks (like you are stomping on a roach) tend to be especially useful here because the distance is so close. If the attacker is behind you, you can follow the stomp with an elbow strike. Bend your arm so that your elbow forms a sharp point, and your upper arm and elbow lie along your rib cage. To prepare to strike, keep your elbow sharply bent as you rotate your arm up around your shoulder joint so that your fingers run through your hair. To strike, rotate your arm back down around your shoulder joint. Your elbow should slide by your ribs and then drive into your attacker. (Remember that you don't want to hit your target with your elbow, you want to drive your elbow clean through your target.)

I mentioned this in chapter 8, but it's just as pertinent here. Never go with anyone who's attacking you, even if they have a gun. They want to take you someplace where it will be easier for them to hurt you. They are more likely to kill you if they kidnap you and take you someplace more private than they are in a public space, because there is less risk of getting caught.

If someone points a gun at you, breathe and stay calm. Trust your instincts. Act submissive and calmly ask the attacker what he or she wants. If the attacker wants your wallet, jewelry, or some other material possession, give it to him or her. Material objects are not worth risking your life.

If the attacker indicates that he or she wants to hurt you, remain calm and keep the attacker talking. There are several options that may improve your odds of getting away. One option is to calmly but authoritatively order the attacker to put down the gun, speaking to the attacker as you would to a child that's doing something inappropriate. This tactic actually has worked for women against potential rapists. Another tactic is to make a run for it. Look for an exit, bend over and run in a zig-zag pattern. Bending over makes your butt the most obvious target, and it's better to be shot in the butt than anyplace else. Zig-zagging makes you more difficult to hit. If you can, get things like cars or columns between you and the gun.

If you are shot, don't give up. You probably will feel a deep, burning, painful sensation and then experience a stunning shock. Do your best to ignore the pain and keep fighting or running away. You have a 75% chance of surviving a handgun wound. But if you quit, there is a chance that your assailant will keep firing, perhaps landing a fatal bullet[69].

Defending Yourself with Weapons

Ordinary Objects as Weapons

While weapons do not have magical capabilities, they can improve your defensive capabilities. Sharp objects such as pencils, keys, scissors, and screwdrivers can be used to poke someone in the eye. Small dense objects such as rocks, paperweights, rolls of quarters, markers, and small flashlights can be used to make a more solid fist to strike the temple, bridge of nose, jaw, or groin. Blunt objects such as bats, canes, sticks, logs and flashlights can be used like a baseball bat to strike an attacker. Vases and lamps can be thrown to break a window to attract attention.

Just about anything can be used as a weapon, but some objects make better weapons than others. In general, blunt weapons are better than sharp weapons at stopping an attack. Blunt weapons shock the body, making it hard to move. If you've ever bumped into the edge or corner of a piece of solid furniture, you've felt the stun potential of blunt weapons. Blunt weapons have this sort of stunning potential, but the effect of the blow is amplified by the speed to the strike.

One of the best, all-purpose ordinary object weapons available is a flashlight, made from anodized aluminum like the police often use, such as a Maglight[70] or Kel-lite. Loaded with batteries, these flashlights pack quite a punch. Maglights loaded with D-cell batteries are quite heavy and swing like a lead pipe. If you have small hands or do not have strong wrists, get a Maglight that uses C-cell batteries instead. This smaller version will still pack a punch but will be easier to swing.

It is important to practice striking with your Maglight if you intend to use it as a weapon. The first step is to hold the Maglight correctly. Hold the Maglight like the police hold their flashlights, near the bulb end, with fingers all touching each other and your pinkie and ring finger wrapped around the bulb end and your thumb, index and middle fingers wrapped around the base of the shaft. If you hold the flashlight at the bottom end and strike with the bulb end, the flashlight will be easy to grab and wrest from your hand.

The easiest way to strike with a Maglight, stick, pipe, or other blunt object is to swing it like a baseball bat, throwing your whole body into the swing. You can strike the head, jaw, neck, elbow, and ribs with this strike. A second easy way to strike with a blunt weapon is to cross your swinging arm across your chest so that your elbow is near your hip bone and your hand is floating over your heart and your weapon is almost touching the edge of your shoulder. To strike, extend your hand out as if you were striking with your fist. You can snap your wrist at the end of the arm extension if you'd like. Good targets for this strike are the head, jaw, neck, elbow, and ribs. A third way to strike with a blunt weapon is to strike down with it as if it were an ax. Aim for the collarbone.

It is important to remember that weapons can be dangerous. Do not use any sort of weapon if you do not feel that you need to inflict harm on someone in order to get away. For example, a blow to the temple with one of these flashlights or a lead pipe can be fatal, and a strike to the shin is likely to cause a fracture[71].

Practice is the key to using weapons as self-defense. While it is possible to use a random object to defend yourself, your ability to really make that weapon work for you will increase if you practice with it or with something similar[72].

Finally, no weapon will do you any good if it's not accessible when you need it. A weapon that you have to dig for in your purse or backpack is virtually useless. You can't ask someone who is about to attack you to wait while you dig through your bag for a weapon. And if you do have time to dig through your bag for a weapon, you probably have time to get away.

Knives and Guns

You may have noticed that although I have been talking about weapons, I have not talked about using knives and/or guns to defend yourself. The reason is that knives and guns are not very good weapons for most people. Both require a great deal of training and practice and are fraught with ethical and legal issues.

Knives in particular are not very good self-defense weapons unless you are really good with them. First, they do not have much stun potential. A cut will hurt eventually, but it may take a long time before that pain is incapacitating. Second, there are not many really good targets. The ribs and skull tend to protect the brain, heart and lungs. And most knives are too short to do significant damage to the kidneys or other organs. The best target is the throat, but this is probably lethal. In order to really use knives to their full potential, you need to train with them in a focused, dedicated manner.

Guns are better self-defense weapons than knives, but there are number of considerations that may make them less than ideal self-defense weapons.

If anyone in your house either suffers from depression or has a bad temper, you should not own a gun. In either case a readily accessible gun could be deadly[73].

If there are children in your home, you need to think hard before you choose to buy a gun for self-defense purposes. Firearms and children have proven to be a disastrous combination. According to the Center to

Prevent Handgun Violence, gun-related accidents were the fifth-leading cause of accidental death for children under 15 in 1991[74]. In order to prevent accidents of this sort from happening, you need to keep the gun and the bullets both locked up in separate rooms[75]. Unfortunately, this safety precaution renders your gun all but useless as a defensive weapon.

If you do not keep your gun clean and in good working order, practice with it often, take it every place you go, and/or are not willing to kill someone with it, the only thing that owning a gun will give you is a false sense of security.

Owning a gun for self-defense purposes requires that you radically alter your lifestyle. In order for a gun to be a useful weapon, you must have it with you in an easily accessible place and be conscious of it at all times. In some respects, it is like having a small child that you must constantly think about. In addition, it is illegal to carry firearms where alcohol is served. This means that you cannot take your gun with you when you go out to bars to dance, drink, and socialize, and therefore will not have it with you when you go to or leave the bar if you happen to be attacked. Not only do guns require mental energy, they require time. In order to be proficient, you need to practice shooting your gun at least once a month. In addition, you need to clean it regularly and check to make sure that it's in good working order.

Finally, you need to ask yourself the following questions: are you willing to kill someone with a gun, and are the benefits of owning a gun worth the risk of accidentally killing an innocent bystander, your lover, or your child with your gun? If you answered no to either of these questions, you should not own a gun.

If after weighing all the pros and cons of gun ownership you do decide to buy a gun for self-defense purposes, make sure that you buy one with sufficient stopping power. The Saturday-night-special types of guns are not very good for self-defense purposes because unless you hit a deadly target, the bullets don't cause much immediate stunning physical shock to the body. As with knives, a person can be hit and bleeding and still keep coming at you. Many gun experts consider the .38 Special to be "the bottom-line minimum for 'stopping power' against a violent antagonist[76]." In order to have ample stun potential, a gun must be 32 caliber or higher.

Finally, make sure that you comply with licensing requirements and other gun laws in your state. You may find yourself facing jail time if you violate gun laws in order to defend yourself, even if you can prove that you were acting in self-defense.

Self-Defense Law Revisited

In the eyes of the law, it doesn't matter if you hit someone with a billy-club or a paper weight. If you have hit someone hard enough to cause injury, you have assaulted someone unless you can show that you were acting in self-defense. Further, the law considers intent to be important. So if the counsel for the opposing side can prove that you were carrying the object that you used to defend yourself with the purpose to hit someone, a judge or jury might construe this as malicious intent on your part. Using something ordinarily construed as a weapon such as a knife or gun in self-defense may be construed to imply that your actions were more offensive than defensive. In addition, the law frowns upon those who carry guns without a license or otherwise carry them illegally. Similarly, if you tell a police officer or other member of the legal system that you were carrying the flashlight as a weapon, it will be seen as a weapon in the eyes of the law. The same goes for other objects in your environment that are not ordinarily thought of as weapons.

In order to avoid this legal loophole, it is important to avoid saying, "This is my weapon." If you are carrying an ordinary object to use as a weapon, remind yourself and the police of its ordinary purpose. You may have a roll of quarters in your pocket for laundry or to feed the soda machine. You may have a flashlight either because it is dark or because you knew that it would get dark at some point.

Exercises

There is little doubt that weapons, especially guns, knives and blunt objects, increase the danger of an attack. However, statistics indicate that the risk of being killed in a weapons attack is pretty low for two reasons.

First, most attacks don't involve weapons. Second, most people survive attacks even when weapons are involved.

At the same time, you can improve your odds of getting away with as little harm to yourself as possible by using a weapon to defend yourself, if you use that weapon properly. This chapter covered both the odds of being attacked with weapons and surviving those attacks and how to use weapons to defend yourself. The next chapter covers same-sex intimate violence. The exercises that follow will help you to expand your ability to defend yourself against an armed assailant and to use weapons in self-defense. Remember that it's great to practice with a partner, but remember that you never want to practice full force blows or at full speed with a partner, nor do you want to use real weapons. Practice with a partner only in slow motion.

Exercise 10.1. Set aside 30 minutes to practice the following knife defense technique. Stand up and imagine that an attacker has grabbed you from behind so that his or her stomach and chest rubs against your back and has a knife at your throat. Grab the blade with your fingers to keep the blade from cutting your throat. (Your fingers may get cut, but you can live with this. A sliced carotid artery can be lethal.) Note which hand that the attacker is using to hold the knife. You want to attack that side. Glance down to see where the attacker's feet are, and then immediately stomp on the top of the attacker's foot. Immediately after you stomp on the attacker's foot, strike with your elbow, as described earlier in the chapter, while still holding on to the knife with your other hand. Note: If the attacker is holding the knife in his or her right hand, stomp on the attacker's right foot and strike with your right elbow. Follow your elbow strike and turn into the attacker (so that you are going towards the side with the knife) and smash the attacker across the jaw with a left palm heel (see chapter 8). If you can get away at this point, do so. Otherwise, follow that up with a left knee to the attacker's groin. (The motion is the same one that you would use to go up and down a set of stairs, except that you are snapping your knee into the attacker's groin as if it were a football you were trying to kick through a goal post.)

Exercise 10.2. Look around your everyday environment for things that you could use to defend yourself, and then practice striking with them. With sharp objects, visualize striking an attacker's eyes. With small, hand-held blunt objects, practice your punches from Chapter 8, visualizing striking your attacker in the nose, jaw, throat or groin, and get used to how each object feels. With blunt objects like a Maglight flashlight, bat, club or stick, practice the strikes discussed earlier in the chapter.

CHAPTER 11
When Love Feels More Like Hate:
Getting Out of an Abusive Relationship

So far, I have focused on self-defense against hate crimes—crimes directed at us from the outside world. This chapter takes a turn inward and focuses on intimate violence—- violence that strikes from inside the community, inside our hearts and our homes.

The strategy for defending yourself in an abusive relationship in some ways mirrors the self-defense strategies in anti—GLBT attacks: the best and surest strategy is prevention. This requires awareness and attitude early on. In order to avoid getting sucked into an abusive relationship, you have to tune in and listen to your gut and be willing to leave if something doesn't feel right. The more involved you get with someone, the harder it is to hear what your intuition tells you about that person. This is especially the case if you are emotionally vulnerable for any reason.

In order to use your intuition, you have to be willing to believe that someone that you are attracted to, someone you trust enough to go out with, would hurt you. You also have to be willing to get out of the relationship if your intuition gives you signals. Once abuse has started, the ultimate self-defense option is to leave. You can love someone all you want, but you have to love yourself more and get yourself out that door to safety, even if it means traveling across the country, leaving everything else behind.

It's easy for most of us to recognize and acknowledge hate crimes directed towards the GLBT community as violence. The singed rainbow flag hanging from the front porch, epithets such as "faggot" and "dyke" yelled in a menacing way from a passing car, the hate-charged beating, the bombing of the gay bar: these are all easily recognizable as acts of hate.

Same-sex intimate abuse is often more difficult to recognize early on, at least from the inside. For example, Sylvia, a "high femme" leather dyke with a prestigious professional career, had a partner, Marti, who monitored her every moment and at one point threw her through a plate glass window. She points out how the gradual nature of the abuse made it hard to recognize at first:

> I didn't realize what was going on in my life. It happened piece-by-piece, moment-by-moment. It became normal. I did not see it as abuse. I didn't even know it until I got out.

Abuse often starts discretely as something that can be explained and dismissed. This makes trusting one's intuition all the more difficult. For example, Chris, a lesbian in her thirties living in a Midwestern metropolitan city, describes how the ambiguous nature of her partner's behavior made it difficult to clearly label as abuse:

> There were a couple of times when we were working out together [practicing martial arts].... There was a certain kind of physical contact that was happening that I felt was really ambiguous. She punched me pretty hard a couple of times in a way that could be dismissed as accidental or screwing around or as miscalculating, but also were pretty unusual for someone who had that kind of training. There was something about these little accidents that made me feel like they weren' t really accidents. They were just a little too rough. But again, when you're practicing martial arts with someone, it's often the case that people do miscalculate, that you can get bruised, although I had been doing this stuff for a while and had never gotten hurt. So I was a little surprised when roughhousing with her actually did get little rough.

Abusers themselves add to the sense of ambiguity. They have a vested interest in defining their behavior as something other than abuse. Abusers also can be good at finding a way to explain the abuse that makes the recipient feel either crazy for thinking it's abuse or responsible for making the incident happen. Chris describes her partner's response when Chris called her on her potentially abusive behavior:

When I would call her on these types of incidents, she would say that it was really being hypersensitive on my part. Or when I would compare this to if a man did this to a woman, in the context of a heterosexual example, she would say, 'Listen, the power between women is equal so this is not abusive if I do this. Yes, if a man did that, I could certainly see that that was out of line. But since women are in equal power relationships, there's nothing wrong with that. First of all, I meant it as a joke. Second, I would never hit you. And third, that kind of stuff happening between women is not the same as stuff that happens between heterosexuals.'

Chris describes her struggle between trusting her gut and trusting her partner:

[My gut told me that [her explanation] was crap. But when you're in a relationship with somebody, you want to trust them. And I have been told, "You're hypersensitive." And I've got all this self-defense training. Maybe I'm just more in tune to this kind of thing than most people are. It's easy not to trust your instincts because of all these reasons, and because all of this is so ambiguous. It's easy to say to yourself, 'Ok, maybe this was a joke. Ok, maybe those missteps while we were roughhousing really were missteps."

Signs of Abuse

Though some of the signs of abuse can be confusing and ambiguous, there are a number of clear warning signs for intimate abuse. Physical violence, of course, is the most obvious sign. If your partner slaps, hits, beats, restrains, or throws you through a plate glass window; throws you down the stairs or over a balcony; or points a gun at you; your abuse detector should be beeping loudly enough for the neighbors to hear.

As discussed in chapter three, other signs of intimate abuse are emotional putdowns, jealousy, forced isolation, emotional explosions, and threats of self-harm. Another sign that should set your abuse detector off is feeling like you are walking on eggshells around your partner. The people that I interviewed all described making heroic efforts to try to keep their partners from exploding. For example, Ron, a college student when the relationship began, describes his efforts to keep the peace.

> I would make sure there was always food ready when he got home…When we got up in the morning I would get up before he got up and get ready so I would look presentable for him when he got up. Anything that he pretty much wanted, any desire, I would do for him, baby him so to speak, just to make sure that he didn't have any reason to get mad.

Similarly, Sylvia explains her efforts to avoid an outburst.

> [I] literally would vacuum 3 times a week, would look at the carpet and check it 20 minutes before she came home, making sure it was all going directionally in the same way.… I developed a sense of anticipation. Anything that had ever caused screaming, hitting, yelling, sexual abuse, rape, any of that…I tried to do everything and make it perfect to somehow stave off the reaction.

Amy, a college student when she got involved with her abuser, puts it more succinctly. "The relationship became a series of me saying what I needed to say to keep her from freaking out."

Another sign that Mr. or Ms. Wonderful isn't quite as good as they seem is that they ridicule or humiliate you. For example, Amy recalls, "She would pay attention to every little word I said, and pick at me about things that I said wrong." Joe, a young, gay man living on the East coast, recounts a similar experience. "I think he purposely built me up in his eyes so that he could tear me apart whenever he felt like it." Joanna, a lesbian in her mid—twenties living in the rural Midwest, describes more patterned emotional abuse: "Every night before she left for work, I had to go out and sit with her, for an hour, to have a bitch fest. She would bitch at me for an hour about everything that I had done wrong that day."

Control over where you go, whom you go with and how long you're gone, or jealousy (often these two are a package deal) should also set off your abuse detector. Jealousy and control can set up a situation of isolation, which makes getting out very difficult. As Joanne describes, sometimes control can begin subtly.

> My best friend had come to visit. She lived in a big city and she wanted me to go home with her and party. And I was like, 'Well, I would, but I'm kinda with somebody right now, and I need to check in and see what they think.' She was like, 'What do you mean you need to check in? You ain't never had to check in with nobody.' And I was like, 'Well, this is different.'

Joanne explains why she felt that she had to check in.

> If I said, 'I want to go to the store.' She said, 'Ok, I'll go with you.' Or 'Ok, why don't you take one of the kids.' It didn't matter where I went, from the very beginning. Either we did it together, or I took a kid or her mother. It just sort of filtered in, and all a sudden, I thought, 'I have to ask.'

Of course, when their subtle control is challenged, abusers often take steps to make their control clear. For example, Joanne describes what happened when she challenged Celia's control:

> She said, 'You're not going down there....' The argument just progressed. That's the first time she slapped me. She was like, 'You're not listening to me. I'm telling you you're not going. If we're going to be together, you're not going to be out running the street, fucking all these people.' She was just screaming at me. That's the first time she ever said anything about thinking that I might cheat on her.

Abusers may also use emotional manipulation to keep their partners under their thumb. Sylvia's explains how Marti manipulated her in to staying home.

> When I went to do this [go out by myself] and begin living my normal life, if you will, she [said] to me, 'Please don't. When you leave, the house becomes so quiet [that] it reminds me of

when Betsy died and the silence terrorizes me.' And so I'm thinking, 'Oh my god, I'm thinking about going out for an hour, to have a drink, to just watch strangers and amuse myself. How selfish can I be against this woman's terror?

It wasn't enough to keep Sylvia at home with her, Marti wanted Sylvia home all the time. Sylvia describes how Marti accomplished this goal.

I got a superb job, earning great money again. She started showing up at the job and calling. And I told her, 'Look, darling, you cannot do this. You don't understand. The boss can't get away with this.' I actually got fired.

After getting Sylvia fired, Marti convinced her not to get another job. Once Sylvia was no longer working, Marti basically kept her under house arrest.

I got further isolated and ended up in a situation where normal life for me [meant that] she would call every 30 minutes. If I had errands to run, I would literally tell her, 'I'm going to the dry cleaner, to the grocery store, to the hardware store, the plant store for this and then I'll be back.' And she would say, 'Ok, that should take about an hour and forty-five minutes.' Damned if [when] I walked through the door, the phone would be ringing. It gives 'trophy femme' a whole new meaning....

Joe's partner Jimmy found different way to keep him virtually imprisoned.

Well, after [Jimmy] graduated, his possessiveness multiplied. Even though we didn't even go to the same high school, he felt that he would see me less and got more suspicious and jealous of what I may have been doing when he wasn't around. He bought ME a present when he graduated—a pager and a cell phone—so that he could reach me whenever he wanted, and I would have no excuse for not responding. He insisted on me wearing it to school, even though he knew it would have gotten me suspended.

Sexual abuse is another signal that should set off your abuse detector. If your partner doesn't respect your boundaries, hurts you (without consent) or disregards your safe words, your abuse detector should be beeping persistently and loudly. Joe describes the pattern of sexual abuse in his relationship:

> [Jimmy] had been, from the start, just a bit more physically comfortable than most people would be at that early stage, but what did I know? He was extremely aggressive when making love, and when in the act, he would often ignore my complaints about being uncomfortable or in pain. He was also a very self-centered lover, but it was my first time, so I took it that it would come in time...He was almost vicious in the bedroom. I would cry sometimes, and he never paid any attention.

Please remember that if at any point during a sexual encounter you wish to stop, you have a right to say, "Stop," in some fashion or another. The person/people that you are involved with must stop. Sexual assault laws vary from state to state, but at a moral level, anything that happens without consent is a sexual violation. For a more complete list of abuse signs, check out: "Men Who Beat the Men Who Love Them" and "Lesbians Talk Violent Relationships[77]."

Patterns of Abuse

Abuse may start as ambiguous and discrete, but once abusers learn that they can get away with it, they tend to escalate their abusive behavior. Sylvia describes how her partner gradually became more abusive and how she learned to accept that abuse:

> Naturally, she learned. She would do something—Let's stick it on a scale of one to 50. She did something at the beginning that was a five. It worked. She did another 5. It worked faster. Then

she stepped up to a 7. Everything progressive. It's a mutual grooming if you will. I learned to adapt to it slowly because that was my environment. She learned to do it because she could, and so she did.

In addition to gradually escalating their abusive behavior and challenging any accusation of wrongdoing, most abusers tend to, at least at first, make extravagant efforts to make up for their behavior. Lenore Walker calls this the honeymoon phase of an abuse cycle. This warm, loving behavior makes the dynamics of the relationship confusing. The efforts that abusers take to make up for their abuse often give their partners hope that the abuse will not happen again; that this warm, loving phase is what the relationship is all about. For example, Joe describes Jimmy's efforts to make up for the abuse and their effect on him.

[After he hit me the first time], nothing was the same. It's not like the next day he began to beat me on schedule or anything. But it DID set a precedent. The first time, not only did he not apologize, [but] he never even acknowledged it happened. I was afraid to bring it up. Every time after that, though, there was always this huge production meant to get me to take him back...despite the fact that I never once told him I'd never see him again.... It was like our first date all over again. In fact, quite a few times, he took me to the same restaurant we went to the first time we went out together. I guess it was supposed to bring back good memories.... Really, it was such a big deal: flowers, dinner, the Jimmy I fell in love with all over again.

Sometimes abusers not only shower their partners with symbols of love, they also use emotional manipulation to keep their partners from leaving. Abusers often, for example, rationalize their jealousy and control as a sign of how much they love and need their partners. They are also prone to using their own past emotional hurts as a ploy to both excuse their abusive behavior and manipulate their partners into staying with them. Joanna's partner Celia combined all of these tactics.

After the first slap, she got up early and went to the store before I even woke up. When I woke up, she had bought me a new pair of tennis shoes. And she was like, 'I love you. I'm sorry about what happened last night. I don't want you to go to the city and find somebody else, because you are so different from anybody I've ever dated before. I've been through a lot in my life and you know what happened to my brother [who had recently been murdered]. And you came into my life at a really, really vulnerable time. And I need you to be here with me.

Although an abuser may make the recipient feel special, giving tokens of affection like roses, romantic dinners, or gifts are standard ploys of abusers. If a manual existed on how to abuse your partner and get him or her to stay with you, that ploy would no doubt be the subject of chapter three, right after the chapters on how to break your partner emotionally and how to effectively isolate your partner.

Romantic gestures are just that: gestures. They do not indicate a concrete will to change. If your partner hits you or attacks you emotionally and then buys you wine and roses, but does not work to deal with her or his problem, then it's very likely that he or she will continue to use you as their emotional and/or physical punching bag. You cannot change them. The only way to get out of this cycle is to leave.

Getting Out

Theoretically, leaving a bad relationship is easy. All you have to do is pack a few things, walk out the door and never come back. Unfortunately, reality seldom runs as smoothly as theory. For starters, it's very likely that the emotional connection is still there. It's very difficult to just walk out on someone you love. Joe describes how love and romance made it hard for him to want to leave.

When we were alone, he was my prince again. We would hold hands and talk about things you never admit to other people. It was pure romance. I've never met a man who can come close to Jimmy when it comes to making me feel so special.

Further, the dynamics of abuse often makes leaving more terrifying than staying. Joe explains,

> There was also the fear of being alone that drew me to him. He really was the only thing I had in the world. Without him, well, let's just say that I was not willing to be without him if I could help it.... Being without him was more frightening than being with him.

Obstacles are another factor that make walking out a challenge. Not all battered women's shelters are equipped to handle lesbian relationships, and there are few, if any, shelters for battered men. The police, emergency room attendants and other service providers may either assume that abuse is something that only happens in heterosexual relationships and not see it when they come in contact with battered lesbians, transgendered people and gay men, or they may simply not respond to intimate abuse appropriately in any circumstance. For example, Chris and her partner went to see a lesbian therapist. The therapist's response to Chris's concerns about abuse was less than supportive.

> The therapist, much to my amazement, said, 'Look, she was just expressing her frustration. She didn't hit you. She didn't throw the wrench.... so get over it.'

In addition, reaching out to service providers involves coming out to them, which for many people, is terrifying and in some cases involves other risks as well.

Abusers themselves create the biggest obstacle to leaving. Many abusers control their partner's money as well as their time so that it's very difficult to get away. Abusers are also likely to stalk their partners, try to frighten them into coning back, or punish them for leaving. For example, the second time that Joanne left her partner, she moved across the country. Her partner tracked her down, kidnapped her at gunpoint and literally held her hostage for over a year.

Although these and many more obstacles may exist, leaving is always an option. All of the people who shared their stories in this chapter, including Joanne, got away from their abusive partners. Leaving was not easy. Several people that I interviewed essentially lived under a system of house arrest. Most feared some sort of violent reprisal. The incidents that follow detail how these people got out.

Making the Decision to Leave

The first part of getting out involves making the decision to leave. Often, this decision is prompted by an escalation of abuse or violence. For example, Ron describes the series of incidents that spurred him to make an escape plan.

> Six months prior to me leaving, he beat me up a lot. I was bruised. Usually he wouldn't hit me in my face. Then he hit me in my face. There was a window in the back of our house, and I had been thrown into it. My head hit it and the window cracked. And then he locked me into a closet and said, 'I'll be back to finish you off in an hour. I'm going out to have a drink.' He never came back that night. [Our housekeeper let me out of the closet, and we sat down and we planned [my escape].

Joe's decision to leave was also instigated by his partner's escalating violence. Joe describes how being thrown down the stairs because he refused to have sex pushed him to think about getting out of the relationship.

> I lost the last bit of control I had in the relationship. The one thing I could always count on, the one weapon I always had, was sex. Not that I controlled him with it, but I always was able to use it...I guess [to] keep him somewhat under control. But after that time, I lost it. I slept with him when he wanted because I was afraid of him; there was no choice left in it. That's when I knew that either I was going to leave or spend the rest of my life with him.

For others, it is a realization about themselves, their partners, or the nature of their relationship that prompts their decision to leave. For example, Sylvia describes how going alone to "the city" (away from her partner's watchful and controlling eye) and spending time with some friends from her past motivated her to leave her partner.

> These two [friends] were having problems. They were things I had worked out a decade before. And I started telling them about everything I had done to insure this, that and the other. I heard myself.... Honestly, when I came back, and I did not come back until 7:00 AM, my partner was fit to be tied. It was so funny. She was standing there at the end of the bed. I was like 'I'm tired, I'm going to sleep,' and she's yelling. I was like, 'You know what, I'm so tired, I can just go to sleep right here and now and you can just keep yelling. Hope it feels good.' I was already like, 'I took an hour to myself and who the fuck does this woman think she is? Look what she's doing to me. Look what's happening in my life. No way. I'm out of here. I'm free....'

You don't have to wait for the mental or physical abuse to become either too frightening or too much to bear. Chris left her partner before she got hit, before verbal abuse pushed her over the edge. She explains what lead her to make the decision to leave.

> Finally, there was an incident that was for me the last straw.... We were going to go to Gay Pride March together and she was going to ride her motorcycle there and be part of the Dykes on Dikes contingent. So we were out in the yard and she was trying to get the motorcycle revved up. She hadn't ridden it for a while and it wouldn't start. So she got out some tools to work on it and it still wouldn't start. And she got very, very frustrated and picked up a very large wrench or hammer and pulled her arm back as if she were going to throw this thing like a baseball. I was probably six feet away from her.... At that point, I ducked and covered my head. It was clear to me that this thing was going to go sailing and I had no idea which direction it was going to go. And I didn't want to have a concussion if it landed on my head. She then didn't let the wrench go. That was pretty

much the point at which I decided these things that I thought were pretty ambiguous, were really clear....

Also, the closer it came to time for me to move in with her, the more frequent these kinds of events became, which also was a very strong warning signal for me.... Once your name is on the lease, or whatever the sign of commitment is, batterers feel like they've got you where they want you and that you can't escape anymore. And I had noticed this happening over time. The closer it came to the point where I wasn't going to have an escape mechanism, the more frequent and overt these kinds of gestures became. And I recognized that for what I thought that was and got out.

Unfortunately, no matter how much you want to believe that your abusive partner will change, that you can love them through their pain and out of their abusive patterns, the truth is that abusers rarely do change, at least not for the better. Typically, they just get more abusive over time. A better belief to cling to is the truth that you deserve to always be treated with respect. Things can be better if you leave your abuser. Life won't be easy and there will be a lot of emotional damage that needs to be repaired and healed, but you can do this work. It's true that you can't change your partner, but you can make changes in yourself, and it won't be as painful as the abuse.

Leaving

Making up your mind to leave is only the first step of the process. In order to get out of an abusive relationship, you actually have to leave. While some people simply pack their bags and say goodbye, it's a good idea to plan your escape. Ron, for example, explains how their housekeeper helped him escape from his partner.

When he would give me money to go buy clothes and things like that for different functions or whatever, he would always give me a lot. She taught me how to just buy exactly what I needed but put money away. She knew what was going on. She helped me save money. She held it at her home. And I left and moved to another city and I didn't tell my parents or anyone. Amy also had help planning her escape.

I had actually come up with a plan about what to do in this sort of situation…. I called my boss and her partner and they came over {with baseball bats} and escorted me out of the house. They {had} told me that I needed to just leave the house, not even acknowledge her, just walk right past her…. When my boss and her partner showed up, {my partner backed} off, like several yards…. I got my stuff together…and they escorted me out of the house…. She asked me for a hug…. I didn't hug her or say anything to her. I just ignored her.

Joanne had to be particularly careful when she left her partner. Celia controlled all of her money and kept track of her almost all of the time. Still, Joanne found a way to get away. First, she found a way to hide some of her money.

[When] I got my first W-2 back and I said, 'I'm just not gonna tell her I got it back….' I hid the W-2 in a leather jacket…. And she asked, 'Where's your W-2?' "I don't know, they haven't given it to me…. Remember last year, we didn't get them 'til the 31st. On the 30th, she said, 'You better go [to work] and see if they're ready, cause if they're not ready, I'm gonna go in there and go off.'

Joanne snuck away the next morning, before Celia could find out about Joanne's W-2 form.

So I went upstairs and threw about five outfits in a trashbag and kinda just waited through the night, cryin' and being scared. Got dressed at 5:00. Took my shower. Acted like I was getting ready for work. Her mom was there cause her mom was always there, watching me. I wrote a short note to Celia just saying,

'I tried my best but I just can't do it. It's over. You can hunt me down, but I'll never be back. This is really it this time.' I threw the bag out the window and went downstairs, like I was leaving [for work] and I left...

After leaving her house, Joanne sought shelter at her best friends' house. She describes how persistently Celia tried to find her.

Soon as [Celia] got off from work, she went to look for me there. I hid in the basement.... It was scary cause she kept coming and coming.... She'd cuss and scream and pound on the door and look in the windows. I would sleep upstairs during the day (at night she was at work and I was pretty sure she wasn't going to lose her job). . As soon as [I heard] the first knock, I'd be down in the basement.

When Celia showed up at the house one night, Joanne's friends invited Celia in to ease her suspicions. The friends got Celia drunk, and after Celia passed out, they helped Joanne to sneak out. Joanne spent the rest of the night and the next day at a neighbor's house. After this, Celia quit stalking the house, but didn't stop looking for Joanne around town. Joanne called her dad to ask him to help her find an apartment in another city before Celia could find her.

[Then] I stayed with a friend in another town.... In the meantime, my dad was getting a vehicle together for me and [finding] me an apartment in another city. So within a week, I had an apartment, a car, and I was on my own. Never went back.

Joe also found a way to disappear. "The summer after I graduated, I went to Paris to stay with a friend who had lived with me as an exchange student. I didn't call or tell Ricky before I left...."

Once You Leave

Unfortunately, leaving you're abusive partner may not be the end of things. Your abuser probably hasn't been particularly respectful of your boundaries in the past and he or she is unlikely to respect them now. She or he may try to woo you back with promises and chocolates, try to scare you back with threats of violence or self-harm, or try to punish you for leaving. This is normal; it would probably be the topic of chapter four of the abuser's manual if such a document existed. For this reason, you need to think very carefully about your strategies for living once you have left your partner.

One strategy is to keep your whereabouts a secret once you leave. The fewer people who know where you are, the fewer people there are who can accidentally or purposefully leak your hiding place to your partner. For example, Joanne didn't even tell her parents where she was at first for fear that Celia would somehow find her. Ron used the same tactic.

It's also a good idea to think about the "what ifs" and come up with strategies on how to deal with them. For example, what will you do if your ex shows up outside your new apartment? What will you do if he or she shows up at the bar, party or other social gathering spot while you're there? What will you do if your ex attacks you on the street or in the hallway of your building, or shows up at your place of employment? These are not fun things to think about, but planning ahead may help you get away from your ex before too much damage is done[78].

It can be very helpful to call the domestic violence shelter in your area to help you work on a safety plan. Moreover, even if they don't have a bed to spare, they may be able to offer you counseling services or support groups to help you heal from the abuse. If your local center isn't helpful, try one of the anti-GLBT violence projects listed in Appendix A.

It may even be helpful to work with the police and the courts to ensure your safety. For example, after Sylvia left, Marti changed the locks on all the doors of their house. The local police actually went with Sylvia to stand guard while she packed her belongings and moved them out of the house.

The police may also be useful in convincing your ex to stop stalking you. For example, Chris was driving with her friend Kim, who had just broken up with an abusive girlfriend. As they were driving, they noticed that Kim's ex, Renee, was following them. (Renee had been stalking Kim since the breakup.) Chris describes how they used the police to get Renee to stop her stalking behavior.

> I knew that there was a police changing station in the neighborhood, so I went there and parked the car. She had followed us and she parked her car. So we went into the police station and said, 'This woman is following us.' So the officers went out and said, 'You're going to have to leave now. You can't be following these women. You've got to know that you're in violation of the law. This woman is telling me that you're stalking her, and if you don't want to be held legally responsible for that, you need to leave now.' So she did. As far as I know, stalking was not a problem after that.

Not only had Renee been stalking Kim, she also owed her a large sum of money that she refused to pay. Rather than let Renee get away with this, Kim took her to small claims court. This was an effective strategy. Chris explains:

> Because the woman didn't want any publicity, she showed up that day with check in hand and settled out of court....

Sometimes relying on the police and the judicial system can be a very effective strategy, but not all abusers will react the same way to police or court intervention. Restraining orders, for example, seem to work well on some abusers but make other abusers even more violent and dangerous. It's important for you to realistically assess how such a move will affect your partner and make your decisions accordingly. If, for example, you feel that taking your partner to court would probably put you at physical risk, it might be a better idea to just cut your losses and run. The same goes with restraining orders and testifying in court. If you are pretty sure that your partner will hurt you or try to kill you after you leave, it might be a good idea to simply disappear like Joanne, Ron and Joe did.

Finally, be prepared to face hostility from either friends, family or service providers. You may be accused of betraying the GLBT community or of breaking your ex's heart. You may also face homophobic responses from service providers. Let that go and remember that you are doing the right thing. You do not ever have to justify your decision to take care of yourself. The simple fact is that you deserve to live without abuse.

For more information on getting out of an abusive relationship, see "Getting Free: You can End Abuse and Take Back Your Life," "Men Who Beat the Men Who Love Them," and "Lesbians Talk Violent Relationships.[79]"

Exercises

Same-sex intimate abuse remains invisible to many people both inside and outside the GLBT community. Nonetheless it's an all too common occurrence. Research suggests that between 25 and 33% of all GLBT intimate relationships involve domestic violence. These rates are comparable to rates of domestic violence among heterosexual couples[80]. The next chapter will discuss ways individuals and groups can counter hate violence and intimate abuse against others in the community. The exercises that follow are designed to help you assess the extent to which your current relationship is abusive and to plan an escape if it is.

Exercise 11.1: Intimate abuse may be difficult to see from the inside, but the patterns are often pretty clear. The following questions are designed to help you assess the extent to which your current relationship is abusive.

Part I: On a scale of one to ten, with one being the lowest and 10 being the highest, to what extent do you:

_____ Feel criticized, putdown, ridiculed, or humiliated by your partner?

_____ Feel like you can't talk to someone or go someplace for fear that your partner will accuse you unjustly of flirting or sleeping around?

_____ Feel like your partner controls your every move?

_____ Feel like you have to walk on eggshells in order to navigate around your partner's moods?

Part II: How frequently have you:

_____ Changed your behavior because your partner threatened to hurt either you or his/herself if you didn't?

_____ Been intentionally shoved, slapped, kicked, or burned by your partner?

_____ Had a child or a pet hurt by your partner?

_____ Had your safe words or boundaries disrespected by your partner during sex?

If your answers in Part I are greater than two, and/or you had any answers above zero in Part II, it is possible that you are in an abusive relationship. Now is as good a time as any to call your local domestic violence shelter or GLBT anti-violence project to discuss your relationship and explore the possibility that you are in an abusive relationship.

Exercise 11.2: If you are in an abusive relationship, contact your local domestic violence shelter or GLBT anti-violence project as soon as you get the chance and have them help you devise a safety plan for leaving your abuser. You may also refer to "Getting Free" and "Men Who Beat the Men Who Love Them[81]."

CHAPTER 12
What Else Can We Do?

The media, especially the gay press, has done a good job of raising our awareness about the issue of anti-GLBT violence. The gay press helped to make our community aware that a problem existed by documenting incidents of violence against GLBT people, and by clearly labeling those incidents for what they are: attacks against us for being members of a group. The gay press also helped to reframe the issue from random, isolated incidents affecting individuals to a patterned social injustice affecting gay, lesbian, bisexual, and transgendered people as a group[82]. In doing so, the press helped to fuel a political movement to criminalize hate crimes[83]. Unfortunately, this focus left many GLBT people feeling overwhelmed, resigned, and afraid.

I started writing this book with the dual intention of challenging this sense of powerlessness, hopelessness and resignation that many of us feel in the face of anti-GLBT harassment and violence and educating the community about same-sex intimate abuse. As the many examples in this book indicate, not only is it theoretically possible to defend ourselves against anti-GLBT harassment and violence and to get out of intimate abusive situations, people are doing it! GLBT people are challenging the messages that say that being a gay, lesbian, bisexual or transgendered person is not okay. GLBT people are confronting harassment at school, at work, in public spaces, and everywhere else, one harasser at a time. GLBT people are taking active measures to defend themselves from physical attacks. GLBT people are getting out of abusive relationships.

Unfortunately, self-defense isn't the same as winning a gold medal at the Olympics. Often the elation of defending ourselves gets over-ridden by whatever the perpetrator said or did and/or by what we should have done. Leaving an abusive or potentially abusive partner may feel especially uncomfortable. Chris, who shared her story of getting out of a relationship before it got abusive in Chapter 11, explains it this way:

It's good to walk away from [a violent relationship], but it's also sad that...you have to end the relationship in order to get some safety. It's hard to get [a] sense of jubilation from that.... Even if you've done good self-defense, that doesn't mean that you're not traumatized by the circumstances or that the circumstances themselves aren't sad that brought you to have to [defend yourself]....

It's important to understand this and to not let the negative feelings about the fact that you had to defend yourself overshadow the positive aspect that you did something to take care of yourself. Hopefully, as you read through the examples in the earlier chapters, you were able to redefine some of your own efforts at self-defense as successful.

At the most fundamental level, gay-bashers and abusive partners harass, abuse and beat us because they can. Until recently, the police did little to deter this violence and in some cases were perpetrators themselves[84]. In order to challenge this violence and abuse, we must fight it both individually and collectively.

Individual Self-Defense

Individually, we need to confront harassment and consciously make choices about how to respond to violence. In intimate relationships, we need to set and maintain boundaries and leave if those boundaries are not respected. In short, we need to defend ourselves. This requires that we be present, aware of our surroundings and tuned in to our intuition so that when our internal alarms go off, we can take action and be willing to defend ourselves if need be.

Awareness and attitude are the most important elements of self-defense, but self-defense techniques can increase both your self-confidence and the options that you have to choose from in any given situation. One very effective way to respond to anti-GLBT harassment is to confront the harasser by defining the situation, interpreting the situation and then telling the offender what to do[85].

Obviously, the best defense against violence is to avoid it altogether. If this isn't possible, research suggests that you can dramatically improve your odds of getting away by employing basic self-defense techniques such as running, yelling, punching and kicking.

In the midst of an attack, remember to keep breathing and to trust your intuition. In some situations, you may avoid or escape an attack by running and/or yelling. In others you may have to punch or kick your attacker in order to get away. In other situations, passive resistance may be the best option. Whatever option you chose, it's important to focus on the fact that you did the best you could with the options that you had and to pat yourself on the back for successfully defending yourself.

Like self-defense techniques, information about weapons can expand your options and self-confidence in the midst of an attack. While weapons can be dangerous, it's important to remember that most attacks don't involve weapons. Even if you are attacked with a weapon, your chances are surviving are pretty good. At the same time, you can improve your self-defense capabilities by using a weapon to defend yourself. Maglight flashlights and other blunt objects are particularly good weapons to use in self-defense because they provide the stunning power needed to stop an attack.

If you are in an abusive relationship, the only self-defense is to get out. Because leaving can be somewhat dangerous, I strongly encourage you to call the GLBT anti-violence program in your area (See Appendix A) or your local domestic violence shelter to seek advice on how best to leave your abuser. Call if you even suspect that you are in an abusive relationship.

If you know someone who is being abused by his or her partner, you have the opportunity to make a difference. Many of the people that I interviewed had help from others to get out. Surprisingly enough, something as simple as the gift of hope can make a big difference. For example, one of Joanne's co-workers had been telling Joanne her story about getting out of an abusive relationship.

> She looked at me and said, 'I know you maybe wonder why I've been telling you this…. You don't have to tell me who you're with. But I'm telling you I see the signs. You're in an abusive relationship. And all I want you to know is to keep the faith and never lose sight of [the fact that] you can get out. It may seem like you can't. It may seem like you're not worthy of anything

better. But you are and you will. I was in a relationship for ten years. I know you know it; I told you enough times. But I'm out. I have a lot less material things now than I ever had. But I'm alive.'

I always think back to that…. When I left, I kept in mind that if she did it after ten years, I could after six.

For ideas on what to do to help a person that you know, call the GLBT anti-violence organization or domestic violence shelter in your area.

Collective Self-Defense

Collectively, we need to work within the political system by making our voices heard about issues affecting our community through phone calls, letters and e-mails to political officials, and most importantly with our votes. We need to support candidates from the local to the national level that promote tolerance and who support our community and campaign against those who don't.

We also need to work outside the system by organizing and participating public protests against the injustices that we face. For example, following the hate-motivated stabbing of a gay University of Arizona student, over 2000 people in Tucson, Arizona marched to protest hate crimes and to demand that officials take this and similar instances seriously[86].

The target of the collective action doesn't always have to be the political system. Sometimes it helps to take action against the perpetrators of anti-GLBT harassment directly. Chris shared the following example about how a chapter of the Lesbian Avengers in the Midwest took on a harasser and ran him out of town.

These dykes…were being harassed by their neighbors. The neighbors were engaged in a variety of actions designed to threaten them, ranging from sending their dog over to knock over their garbage cans and eat their trash to walking around in his living room with his curtain open [while] holding his shotgun in his hand. They tried to get the local sheriff to do something about it, and the local sheriff was in cahoots with him. [The neighbor] did things like calling and leaving harassing messages on the answering machine, and when they asked that a trace be put on their phone, the sheriff clued him in, so he started making calls from pay phones all over the county. This went on for months and months.

Finally, they called the Lesbian Avengers. And the Avengers did a couple of things. One, they went out and picketed this guy. He was an auto mechanic and he owned his own garage.... So they picketed the garage and drew a lot of attention that way. Another thing they did was [go] to the authority that was over the local sheriff with the women. They told them what had been happening and that the local authorities weren't dealing with it appropriately and asked them to investigate it. They got a fabulous response. As a result, enough pressure was put on this guy that he actually sold both his business and his home and moved from the area, and the lesbians are not being hassled any more.

There are obviously many ways to take political action both by working within the political system and by working outside of it. And in many geographical areas, you are probably not alone in your quest to change the system. Many towns and college campuses already have GLBT organizations that can help you find out information about political candidates, rallies, and parades, provide opportunities for you to get involved with the GLBT community and direct you to more specialized groups (such as the Lesbian Avengers, specialized groups for people of color or ACT-UP!) that may meet your needs.

No matter how you chose to defend yourself or how you have defended yourself in the past, remember to honor the choices that you make and to celebrate the fact that you are alive. Obviously you did something right or you wouldn't be reading this! Also, because defending yourself can leave emotional scars, it's important to get support from friends, family and/or counselors if you need it. The bottom line is, no matter what you've done, no matter who you are, no matter what you've grown up believing: you are worth defending!

APPENDIX A

National Coalition of Anti-Violence Projects Member Organizations[87]

* Denote that that project has a domestic violence project as well

Arizona

*Wingspan DV Project
300 East 6th Street
Tucson, AZ 85705
Phone: (520) 624-1779
Website: **www.wingspanaz.org**

Arkansas

*Women's Project
2224 Main Street
Little Rock, AR 72206
Phone: (501) 372-5113
Fax: (501) 372-0009

California

*Community United Against Violence

160 14th St
San Francisco, CA 94103
Phone: (415) 777-5500
Fax: (415) 777-5565
Website: http://www.cuav.org/

Los Angeles Gay & Lesbian Center/Anti-Violence Project
1625 North Schrader Blvd.
Los Angeles, CA 90028
Phone: (800) 373-2227 (victims' line-southern California only)
Fax: (323) 993-7653
Website: www.laglc.org

***Los Angeles Gay & Lesbian Center/STOP Partner Abuse/
Domestic Violence Program**
1625 North Schrader Blvd.
Los Angeles, CA 90028
Phone: (323) 860-5806 (clients)
Fax: (323) 993-7699
E-Mail: domesticviolence@laglc.org
Website: www.www.laglc.org/domesticviolence

*The Lesbian & Gay Men's Community Center, San Diego
P.O. Box 3357
San Diego, CA 92163
Phone: (619) 260-6380, x308
Fax: (619) 260-3092

*W.O.M.A.N., Inc.
333 Valencia Street, #251
San Francisco, CA 94103-3547
Phone: (415) 864-4722, Crisis Line
TTY: (415) 864-4765
Website: www.womaninc.org

Colorado

*Anti-Violence Program
P.O. Box 181085
Denver, CO 80218
Phone: (303) 852-5094
Crisis Line: (888) 557-4441
Phone 2: (303) 839-5204, Office Fax: (303) 839-5205
E-Mail: coavp@hotmail.com
Website: www.coavp.org

Connecticut

Connecticut Womens' Education and Legal Fund
135 Broad Street
Hartford, CT 06105
Phone: 860-247-6090
Fax: 860-524-0804
Website: www.cwealf.org

Illinois

*Horizons Anti-Violence Project
961 W. Montana
Chicago, IL 60614
Phone: (773) 871-CARE, Hotline
Phone 2: (773) 472-6469
Fax: (773) 472-6643
Website: www.horizonsonline.org

Kentucky

Gay & Lesbian Services Organization

PO Box 11471
Lexington, KY 40575-1471
Phone: (606) 257-8462
Fax: (606) 257-5592

Louisiana

Lesbian & Gay Community Center of New Orleans
2114 Decatur
New Orleans, LA 70116
Phone: (504) 945-1103
E-Mail: www.lgccno.net

Massachusetts

*Fenway Community Health Center Violence Recovery Program
7 Haviland Street
Boston, MA 02115
Phone: 1-800-834-3242 (intake line)
Fax: (617) 267-8437 Website: www.fenwayhealth.org

*The Network/La Red
PO Box 6011
Boston, MA 02114
Fax: (617) 695-0877

Michigan

Triangle Foundation
19641 West Seven Mile Road
Detroit, MI 48219

Phone: (313) 537-3323
Fax: (313) 537-3379
Website: www.tri.org

Minnesota

*Out Front Minnesota
310 East 38 Street - Suite 204
Minneapolis, MN 55409
Phone: (800) 800-0127, Hotline
Phone 2: (612) 822-0127
Fax: (612) 822-8786
Website: www.outfront.org

New York

*New York City Gay and Lesbian Anti-Violence Project
240 West 35th Street - Suite 200
New York, NY 10001
Phone: (212) 714-1141, Hotline
Phone 2: (212) 714-1184, Office
Fax: (212) 714-2627
E-Mail: webmaster@avp.org
Website: www.avp.org

Ohio

*Buckeye Region Anti-Violence Organization
P.O. Box 82068
Columbus, OH 43202
Hotline: (866) 86-BRAVO
Phone: (614) 268-9622, Office

Fax: (614) 262-9264, Office
E-Mail: **www.bravo-ohio.org**

*The Lesbian/Gay Community Center
6600 Detroit Avenue
Cleveland, OH 44102
Phone: (216) 651-5428, Center
Fax: (216) 651-6439, Center
Website: **www.lgcsc.org**

Stonewall Cincinnati
PO Box 954
Cincinnati, OH 45201
Phone: (513) 651-2500
Fax: (513) 651-3044
Website: **www.stonewallcincinnati.org**

Oklahoma

Tulsa Oklahomans for Human Rights
4021 South Harvard Avenue - Suite 210
Tulsa, OK 74135-4600
Phone: (918) 743-GAYS (4297)
Fax: (918) 747-5499

ONTARIO

The 519 Anti-Violence Programme
Hotline: (416) 392-6877
www.the519.org

Pennsylvania

The Center for Lesbian and Gay Civil Rights

1315 Spruce Street
Suite 301
Philadelphia, PA 19107
Phone: (215) 731-1447
Fax: (215) 731-1544
Website: **www.center4civilrights.org**

Rhode Island

Rhode Island Alliance for Lesbian and Gay Civil Rights
41 12th Street
Providence, RI 02906
Phone: (401) 331-6671
Phone 2: (508) 897-2040
Fax: (401) 272-4374
E-Mail: **Zeek2k@cs.com**

Texas

*Montrose Counseling Center
701 Richmond Avenue
Houston, TX 77006
Phone: (713) 529-0037
Fax: (713) 526-4367
www.montrosecounselingcenter.org

Vermont

*SafeSpace
P.O. Box 158
Burlington, VT 05402
Phone: (866) 869-7341, Hotline

Fax: (802) 863-0004
Phone 2: (802) 863-0003, office (V/TTY)
Website: http://www.SafeSpaceVT.org

Virginia

Virginians for Justice
P.O. Box 342
Richmond, VA 23218
Phone: (800) 2-Justice, Hotline
Phone 2: (804) 643-4816
Fax: (804) 643-2050
E-Mail: **va4justice@aol.com**

WISCONSIN

Milwaukee Lesbian, Gay, Bisexual and Transgender Community Center
Phone: (414) 271-2656
Website: **www.mkelgbt.org**

ENDNOTES

The Challenge
[1] These headlines were listed in Outlook, May 28-June 10, 1998, in the "Anti-Gay Violence Report."

[2] Outlook, "Anti-Gay Violence Report." Oct, 2-15, 1997, p. 5.

Self-Defense: Defining Our Actions as Successful
[3] Impact self-defense organizations located throughout the United States as well as in Australia, Canada, and Switzerland. To find the impact chapter nearest you via the internet, click on: **www.impactsafety.org/ chapters.htm**

You can find the same information by phone from the United States at 1-800-345-KICK.

Anti-GLBT Violence: Why It Happens and What It Means

[4] Ault took feminist self-defense theory and stretched it to address the needs and experiences of queer people. For more information, see: Ault, Amber, Ph.D. *Self-Defense for Gay, Lesbian and Bi people*, The Ohio State University Rape Education and Prevention Program.

[5] It is important to note that those of us who are female, not of white European decent, differently abled, HIV positive, non-Christian, or different in other ways, may be subject to acts of hatred based on these other statuses in conjunction with or in addition to our queer status.

[6] Clyde W. Franklin II. 1988. *Men and Society*. Chicago: Nelson-Hall.

[7] Clyde W. Franklin II. 1988. *Men and Society*. Chicago: Nelson-Hall.

8. Amber Ault. *Self Defense for Gay, Lesbian and Bi People.* The Ohio State University Rape Education and Prevention Program.

9. See Amber Ault. *Self-Defense for Gay, Lesbian and Bi people*, The Ohio State University Rape Education and Prevention Program. Note: This continuum is not meant to create a hierarchy of trauma but instead is a tool we can use to examine the range of hostility we face as a group. It is possible that someone else would organize the continuum differently.

10. BRAVO Hate Crimes Report. *Outlook*. April 29-May 12, 1999.

11. Island, David and Patrick Letellier. 1991. *Men who beat the men who love them.* New York: Harrington Park Press: P 104.

Awareness: Turning On Your Personal Security System

12. Bloomfield, Harold H. and Robert K. Cooper. 1997. *How To Be Safe In An Unsafe World.* New York: Crown Publishers, Inc.

13. Bloomfield, Harold H. and Robert K. Cooper. 1997. *How To Be Safe In An Unsafe World.* New York: Crown Publishers, Inc.

14. For a more in-depth discussion on relaxed, alert awareness, see Thich Nhat Hanh's (1987) *The Miracle of Mindfulness.* Boston: Beacon Press.

15. Because this is a published account, the names have not been changed.

16. Brenner, Claudia. 1995. *Eight Bullets: One Woman's Story of Surviving Anti-Gay Violence.* Ithaca, NY: Firebrand Books. Pp 20-22.

17. According to police reports, Carr's actions were rooted in deep fear and hatred of homosexuals.

18. See for example: Lejeune, Robert. 1985. "The Management of a Mugging." in James M. Henslin (ed.) *Down to Earth Sociology.* New York: The Free Press; Herek, Gregory M. and Kevin T. Berrill. 1992. *Hate Crimes: Confronting Violence Against Lesbians and Gay Men.* Newbury Park, CA: Sage Publications, Inc.; and Langalan, Martha J. 1993. *Back Off!* New York: Simon and Schuster; Dong, Arthur. 1997. *License to Kill.*

[19] Franklin, Clyde W. II. 1988. *Men & Society.* Chicago: Nelson-Hall.

[20] Dong, Arthur. 1997. *License to Kill.*

[21] None of the men that Dong interviewed were in jail for murdering a lesbian or transgendered person. It is possible that specific justifications for murdering bisexuals, lesbians and transgendered people differ from those for killing gay men. Nonetheless, homophobia lies at the root of all these explanations just as it lies at the root of all anti-GLBT violence.

[22] Dong, Arthur. 1997. *License to Kill.*

[23] Dong, Arthur. 1997. *License to Kill.*

[24] Dong, Arthur. 1997. *License to Kill.*

[25] See for example: Comstock, Gary David. 1989. *Violence Against Lesbians and Gay Men.* New York: Columbia University Press; and Herek, Gregory M. and Kevin T. Berrill. 1992. *Hate Crimes: Confronting Violence Against Lesbians and Gay Men.* Newbury Park, CA: Sage Publications, Inc.

[26] Lejeune, Robert. 1985. "The Management of a Mugging." in James M. Henslin (ed.) *Down to Earth Sociology.* New York: The Free Press: P 228.

[27] Lejeune, Robert. 1985. "The Management of a Mugging." in James M. Henslin (ed.) *Down to Earth Sociology.* New York: The Free Press.

[28] Grayson, B. and M. Stein. 1981. "Attracting Assault: Victim's Nonverbal Cues," *Journal of Communication.* 74.

[29] De Becker, Gavin. 1997. *The Gift of Fear: Survival Signals that Protect Us From Violence.* Boston: Little, Brown and Company.

[30] See for example: Harry, Joseph. 1982. "Derivative Deviance:

The Cases of Extortion, Fag-Bashing, and Shakedown of Gay Men." *Criminology*: 546-564; Comstock, Gary David. 1989. *Violence Against Lesbians and Gay Men*. New York: Columbia University Press; and Dong, Arthur. 1997. *License to Kill*.

[31] Dong, Arthur. 1997. *License to Kill*.

Attitude

[32] Lejeune, Robert. 1985. "The Management of a Mugging." in James M. Henslin (ed.) *Down to Earth Sociology*. New York: The Free Press.

[33] For more information on fear, see: Fein, Judith. 1993. *Exploding the Myth of Self-Defense*. Sebastopol, CA: Torrance Publishing Company.

[34] Bart, Pauline and O'Brian, Patricia. 1985. *Stopping Rape*. New York: Pergamon Press.

[35] Dong, Arthur. 1997. *License to Kill*.

[36] This section refers to U.S. law. Laws on self-defense may differ in other countries.

[37] This is similar to an exercise presented by Shakti Gawain (1982) in *The Creative Visualization Workbook*. San Rafael CA: New World Library.

So What Am I Supposed To Do About It??? Responding To Harassment

[38.] Ault, Amber, Ph.D. *Self-Defense for Gay, Lesbian and Bi People*, The Ohio State University Rape Education and Prevention Program.

[39.] Friskopp, Annette and Sharon Silverstein. 1995. *Straight Jobs, Gay Lives*. New York: Scribner: 318.

[40.] The theoretical ideas presented in this section are based on

Langelan, Martha J. 1993. *Back Off!* New York: Simon and Schuster. Please refer to this work for a more explicit discussion of the history and theory of and guidelines for confrontation from a feminist perspective.

[41.]This three-step model is the one advocated by Amber Ault in *Self Defense for Gay, Lesbian and Bi People.*. The Ohio State University Rape Education and Prevention Program. For a more explicit model see: Martha J. Langalan. 1993. *Back Off!* New York: Simon and Schuster.

5. Not all families will be resistant to your self-empowerment. If your family has always respected your boundaries and applauded you for taking care of yourself even if it means that you are not "nice," they probably will be very supportive of your new assertiveness.

[42.]This excerpt comes from Friskopp, Annette and Sharon Silverstein. 1995. *Straight Jobs, Gay Lives.* New York: Scribner: p 56-57.

[43.]Friskopp, Annette and Sharon Silverstein. 1995. *Straight Jobs, Gay Lives.* New York: Scribner: 125-126.

[44.]Friskopp, Annette and Sharon Silverstein. 1995. *Straight Jobs, Gay Lives.* New York: Scribner: 93-94.

Avoiding Attacks: Why Fight If You Don't Have To?

[45] I use the masculine pronoun, he, because Marla identifies himself as a man who likes to wear women's clothing.

[46] *Outlook.* December 7-20, 2000 (P. 11)

[47] "Two elude carload of men shouting anti-gay slurs in Short North." *Outlook.* April 29-May 12, 1999. (P. 6)

[48] "Gay man threatened by three youths." *Outlook.* June 25-July 8, 1998. (P. 5)

[49] "Lesbian couple harassed at downtown fireworks." *Outlook*. July 9 - 22, 1998.

[50] "Man escapes possible attack." *Outlook*. May 28-June 10, 1998.

Responding to Physical Threats and Assault

[51] Unfortunately, there are no statistics on the effectiveness of resisting anti-GLBT violence. The statistics that we have on anti-GLBT violence are sketchy at best for a number of reasons. First, most GLBT people don't report offenses to police. Second, few law enforcement agencies seriously collect hate crime data. And third, while people are more likely to report a hate crime attack to a GLBT anti-violence organization than to the police, there are very few local GLBT anti-violence projects in the United States. This means that most GLBT people don't have access to a local anti-violence center.

[52] Fein, Judith. 1993. *Exploding the Myth of Self-Defense*. Sebastopol, CA: Torrance Publishing Company.

[53] Pauline B. Bart and Patricia H. O'Brien. 1985. *Stopping Rape*. New York: Pergamon Press.

[54] Dong, Arthur. 1997. "Licence To Kill." San Francisco, CA: Deep Focus Productions.

[55] It's best to practice self-defense techniques with people who don't always have to win. Those sorts of people will be more interested in showing you that they are stronger, tougher, and know more than you than on helping to build your confidence and helping you learn. Chose someone that you trust will give you supportive feedback and help you build your confidence.

[56] "Woman assaulted in Italian Village." *Outlook*. October 30-November 12, 1997. (P. 5)

[57] "Man in brown van decked and arrested" *Outlook*. October 2-15, 1997. (P. 5)

Passive Resistance: Choosing Not to Fight Back

[58] Scarce, Michael. 1997. *Male on Male Rape: The Hidden Toll of Stigma and Shame*. Insight Books: New York (PP xv-xvi).

[59] I do not use a pseudonym in this example because this is a published account.

Weapons

[60] Craven, Diane. 1997. "Special Report: Sex Differences in Violent Victimization, 1994." U.S. Department of Justice Office of Justice Programs, Bureau of Justice Statistics: September 1997, NCJ-164508.

[61] National Coalition of Anti-Violence Programs. 2001. "Anti-Lesbian, Gay, Transgender and Bisexual Violence in 2000." New York. The NCAVP is a coalition of 26 anti-violence organizations that deal with anti-GLBT violence, HIV-related violence and other forms of violence affecting the GLBT community. Of these, eleven organizations collect the detailed data on anti-GLBT incidents occurring in their regions in 1999 and 2000 that are included in this report. (For a list and breakdown of NCAVP programs, please refer to Appendix A.) It is important to note that the NCAVP data analyzed in this chapter are based only on the data collected by these eleven organizations. As such, these data indicate trends in bias-related incidents rather than the actual number of bias-motivated incidents in the United States.

[62] Percentages are rounded to the nearest tenth.

[63] The data on assaults do not include the 28 homicides that happened in 1999 and the 16 that occurred in 2000. It is likely that these homicides involved use of weapons.

[64] National Coalition of Anti-Violence Programs. 2001. "Anti-Lesbian, Gay, Transgender and Bisexual Violence in 2000." New York. (14)

[65] Ayoob, Massad. 1983. *The Truth About Self Protection*. New York: Bantam Books.

[66] Ayoob, Massad. 1983. *The Truth About Self Protection*. New York: Bantam Books.

[67] NCAVP data tallies murders and assaults separately. These odds were found by adding the murders to the total assaults and attempted assaults (725+28 in 1999 and 786+16 in 2000), then calculating the percentage of murders for the total number and rounding to the nearest tenth. The NCAVP data do not indicate whether or not weapons were involved in homicides. Assuming that they were, the probability of being killed if one was attacked with a weapon was 9% in 1999 and 5% in 2000.

[68] Ayoob, Massad. 1983. *The Truth About Self Protection*. New York: Bantam Books.

[69] Maglight flashlights can be found at most hardware stores.

[70] For more information about police flashlights, see: Ayoob, Massad. 1983. *The Truth About Self Protection*. New York: Bantam Books.

[71] For more information about legal issues relating to weapons and self-defense, see: Ayoob, Massad. 1983. *The Truth About Self Protection*. New York: Bantam Books.

[72] For more information about handguns, see Fein, Judith. 1993. *Exploding the Myth of Self-Defense*. Sebastopol, CA: Torrance Publishing Company.

[73] "Facts about Children and Handguns," The Center to Prevent Handgun Violence, Feb. 1991.

[74] See Ayoob, Massad. 1983. *The Truth About Self Protection.* New York: Bantam Books, for information about gunlock systems if you have or plan to have children but are serious about buying a gun.

[75] Ayoob, Massad. 1983. *The Truth About Self Protection.* New York: Bantam Books (P 354).

When Love Feels More Like Hate: Getting Out of an Abusive Relationship

[76] Island, David and Patrick Letellier. 1991. *Men Who Beat the Men Who Love Them.* New York: Harrington Park Press; and Taylor, Joelle, and Tracey Chandler. 1995. *Lesbians Talk: Violent Relationships.* London: Scarlet Press.

[77] Planning ahead doesn't guarantee that you won't get hurt again, but it will help you expand your options.

[78] NiCarthy, Ginny. 1986. *Getting Free: You Can End Abuse and Take Back Your Life.* 2nd ed. Seal Press: Seattle; Island, David and Patrick Letellier. 1991. *Men Who Beat the Men Who Love Them.* New York: Harrington Park Press; and Taylor, Joelle, and Tracey Chandler. 1995. *Lesbians Talk: Violent Relationships.* London: Scarlet Press.

[79] Brand, P.A and A.H. Kidd. 1986. "Frequency of Physical Aggression in Heterosexual and Female Homosexual Dyads." *Psychological Reports.* 59: 1307-1313; Koss, M.P. 1990. "The Women's Mental Health Research Agenda: Violence Against Women." *American Psychologist.* 45: 374-380; Lockhart, L., B. White, V. Causby, and A. Isaac. 1994. "Letting Out the Secret: Violence in Lesbian Relationships." *The Journal of Interpersonal Violence.* 9: 469-92.

[80] NiCarthy, Ginny. 1986. *Getting Free: You Can End Abuse and Take Back Your Life.* 2nd ed. Seal Press: Seattle; Island, David and Patrick Letellier. 1991. *Men Who Beat the Men Who Love Them.* New York: Harrington Park Press.

What Else Can We Do?

[81] Streitmatter, Rodger. 1995. *Unspeakable: The Rise of The Gay and Lesbian Press in America.* Boston: Faber and Faber.

[82] Sewell, Regina. 1997. *Violent Politics and the Politics of Violence: The Criminalization of Anti-Lesbian/Gay Violence* . Dissertation: The Ohio State University.

[83] For example, see: Sewell, Regina. 1997. *Violent Politics and the Politics of Violence: The Criminalization of Anti-Lesbian/Gay Violence* . Dissertation: The Ohio State University; and Kennedy, Elizabeth Lapovsky, and Madeline D. Davis. 1993. *Boots of Leather, Slippers of Gold.* New York: Routeledge, Inc.

[84] This three-step model is the one advocated by Amber Ault in *Self Defense for Gay, Lesbian and Bi People..* The Ohio State University Rape Education and Prevention Program. For a more explicit model see: Martha J. Langalan. 1993. *Back Off!* New York: Simon and Schuster.

[85] Kerr, Mark R. "Tucson, AZ Hate Crime Protested." *__PlanetOut News__*. Tuesday, February 15, 2000.

Appendix A

[86] This list came from a compilation of lists presented on the New York Anti-Violence Project website **http://www.avp.org/** and the National Coalition of Anti-Violence Programs website **http:// www.ncavp.org/**

www.ingramcontent.com/pod-product-compliance
Lightning Source LLC
Chambersburg PA
CBHW071356280526
45787CB00001B/347